The 5-Minute BIBLE STUDY for Women

YOU are the reason we do what we do here at Barbour Publishing. We promise that we will always use our God-given talents to produce content with you in mind—and that we will remain biblically faithful, no matter what.

Thank you for being the heart of our business.

ISBN 979-8-89151-271-9

Published by Barbour Publishing, Inc., 1810 Barbour Drive, Uhrichsville, Ohio 44683, www.barbourbooks.com

Our mission is to inspire the world with the life-changing message of the Bible.

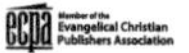

Printed in the United States of America.

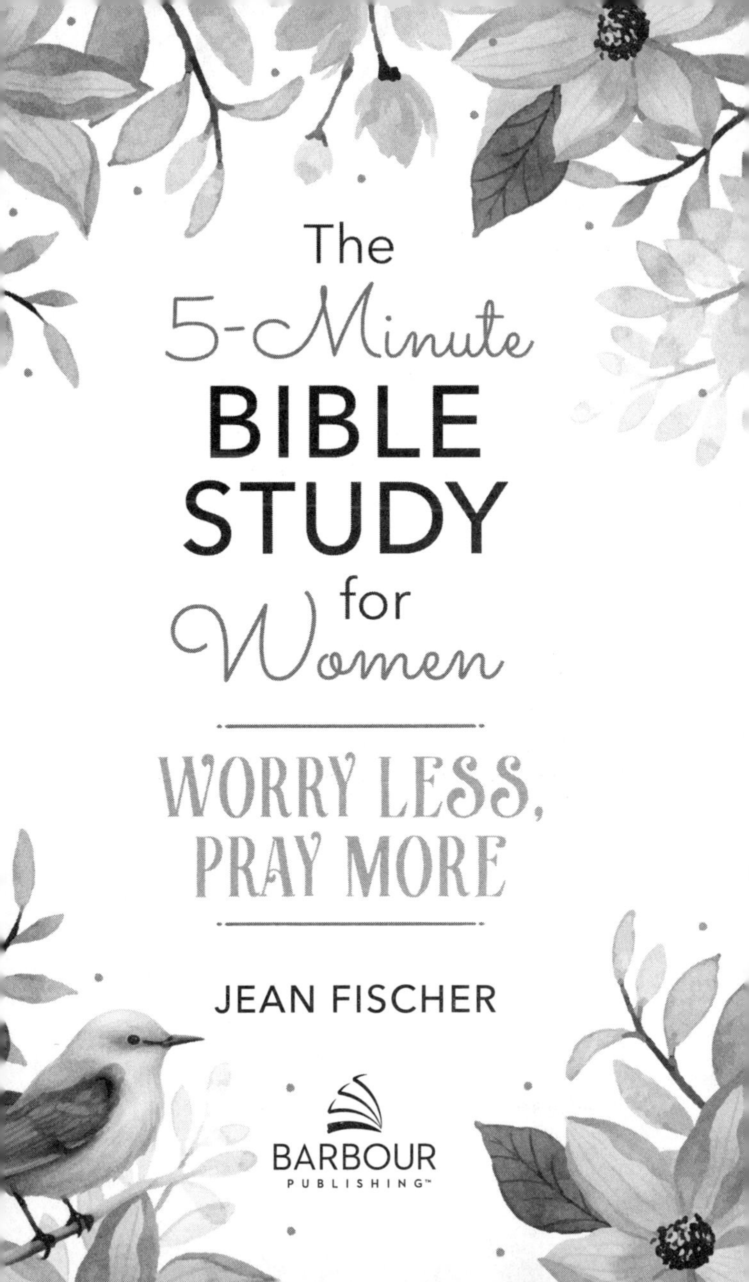

The 5-Minute BIBLE STUDY for Women

WORRY LESS, PRAY MORE

JEAN FISCHER

BARBOUR
PUBLISHING™

INTRODUCTION

Do you worry about finances, relationships, work, trouble in the world. . . ? Let this book guide you toward worry-free living. Even if you have only five minutes each day, studying God's Word and applying it to your life can help you live worry-free.

- Minutes 1–2: ***Read*** carefully the scripture passage for each day's Bible study.
- Minute 3: ***Understand.*** Consider prompts that encourage you to apply the Bible verses and the devotional reading to your life. Reflect on these throughout your day.

- Minute 4: ***Apply.*** Read a brief devotion based on the day's scripture. Think about what you are learning and how to apply what you've learned.
- Minute 5: ***Pray.*** A prayer starter helps you begin a conversation with God. Remember to allow quiet time for Him to speak to your heart as well.

The 5-Minute Bible Study for Women: Worry Less, Pray More will help you form a habit of studying and applying God's Word. Make the first five minutes of your day count! Pour yourself a cup of coffee and dig in. You will discover that even five minutes of focused scripture reading and prayer can make a huge difference in reducing your worries.

GOD'S PROMISE

Read Isaiah 41:10–13

Key Verse:

"For I am the Lord your God Who holds your right hand, and Who says to you, 'Do not be afraid. I will help you.'"
ISAIAH 41:13 NLV

Understand:

- What are you most afraid of?
- How do you find peace when you feel worried or afraid?

Apply:

Imagine a world without worries or concerns, a place free from anything that could frighten you. We can look forward to that in heaven. But we aren't there yet. We live in a sin-filled world rife with challenges and obstacles. Allowing them to occupy our thoughts leads to worry and fear. The good news is we can find peace amid the chaos when we learn to trust in God's goodness and His mighty power.

In Isaiah 41:10–13, God tells us not to be afraid. He reminds us that He is with us. God says, "*For sure* I will help you" (verse 10 NLV, emphasis added). That is a promise to us, and God keeps every one of His promises. Whatever trouble we face, we can be *sure* He will help us get through it.

As you read and think about God's Word, you will find yourself growing nearer to Him and understanding that His faithfulness is greater than your worries. With God holding your hand, you can face your fears with strength, knowing that He will fight for you. Think of His goodness and love today. God is reaching out His hand to you. Take it! Follow Him, and He will lead you to peace that is beyond your understanding.

Pray:

Yes, Lord, I will take Your hand. May Your mighty power extend through me and give me courage and strength to face whatever obstacles get in my way.

WHY DO WE WORRY?

Read Genesis 3

Key Verses:

Then the Lord God said, "See, the man has become like one of Us, knowing good and bad. Now then, he might put out his hand to take from the tree of life also, and eat and live forever." So the Lord God sent him out from the garden of Eden, to work the ground from which he was taken.

GENESIS 3:22–23 NLV

Understand:

- God created us to be free. What does that mean to you?
- How could your day be different if you made a conscious effort to obey God?

Apply:

Eden was heaven on earth. Worries, concerns, and suffering didn't exist. If Adam and Eve had obeyed God's rule not to touch that one tree, we could be living forever in harmony and peace. But their disobedience opened the door to evil. Adam and Eve realized they could choose bad over good, and they chose bad.

God didn't create us to be His slaves. He gave us freedom to make our own choices. When Adam and Eve chose to disobey, they broke their relationship with God. Their choice unleashed sin in the world, and that affected all humanity. As the world's population grew, more and more people chose sin over obedience. The consequence was worry, fear, and suffering forever. But because God loves us, He didn't want that. He also didn't want us to die for our sins. So God planned to save us from sin and provide us forever life with Him in heaven. He sent us a Savior—Jesus.

Pray:

Dear God, every day I am tempted to disobey You. When I give in to sin, You love me anyway. Thank You for sending Jesus to restore my relationship with You. Thank You for not giving up on me.

OUR SAVIOR

Read John 3:16–21

Key Verse:

"For God so loved the world that He gave His only Son. Whoever puts his trust in God's Son will not be lost but will have life that lasts forever."

John 3:16 NLV

Understand:

- What does the word *atonement* mean?
- How can you attain forgiveness for your sins now and forever?

Apply:

In the Old Testament, people atoned for their sins by killing one of their best animals on an altar as a sacrifice to God. The animal that was considered the purest of all was the lamb. The shedding of its blood was a way of temporarily receiving God's forgiveness and being reconciled with Him. These acts would later be seen as a symbolic foreshadowing of Jesus' death on the cross. God sacrificed His best—His only Son, Jesus—shedding His blood as a permanent way of repairing our relationship with Him. Jesus suffered all the consequences of our sins, past, present, and future, so we could be pure enough to enter heaven. If we believe this, we are promised eternal life.

Believing that Jesus is our way to eternal life is a choice. The book of John says some will choose not to believe because they love sin and evil. Others will not believe because they are afraid God will punish them if their sins are exposed. But God already knows our sins. Jesus has already taken the punishment for them. So confessing our sins to God results in just one thing—forgiveness forever. Because we are forgiven, we have nothing to worry about or fear. Jesus, the Lamb of God, is our Savior. Not only will He save us from the punishment of sin, but He will save us from every worry and fear, if only we trust Him.

Pray:

Dear Jesus, help me to be firm in my belief that through You all my sins are forgiven. Remind me that You aren't just my Savior but also the one I can trust.

ONE DAY AT A TIME

Read Matthew 6:25–34

Key Verse:

"Do not worry about tomorrow. Tomorrow will have its own worries. The troubles we have in a day are enough for one day."
MATTHEW 6:34 NLV

Understand:

- What do you most often think about as you lie in bed wanting to sleep?
- What can you do at bedtime to turn your thoughts from worries and concerns?

Apply:

Did you lie awake last night unable to sleep because a bazillion thoughts barreled through your head? Maybe you replayed something unpleasant that happened and you imagined what you could have said or done. Were you thinking about how to stretch your paycheck or about an important decision you need to make? Maybe last night you worried about today.

In the Sermon on the Mount, Jesus told the crowd, "The troubles we have in a day are enough for one day." He offered some examples of things we worry about, and then Jesus said, "So do not worry, saying, 'What shall we eat?' or 'What shall we drink?' or 'What shall we wear?' For. . .your heavenly Father knows that you need them. But seek first his kingdom and his righteousness, and all these things will be given to you as well" (Matthew 6:31–33 NIV). The takeaway, the most important idea Jesus wanted the crowd to remember, was this: Give all your worries to your heavenly Father!

Taking things day by day can help you get a good night's sleep. Form a bedtime ritual of giving all your worries to God. Say this verse to yourself as soon as you lie down: "I will lie down and sleep in peace. O Lord, You alone keep me safe" (Psalm 4:8 NLV).

Pray:

Father, tonight, I give all my thoughts to You. I know You have everything I worry about under control. In the safety of Your presence, I can sleep in peace.

TODAY IS A NEW DAY!

Read Psalm 118

Key Verse:

This is the day that the Lord has made.
Let us be full of joy and be glad in it.
Psalm 118:24 NLV

Understand:

- What do you have to be glad about today?
- What are some ways God has been faithful to you?

Apply:

Good morning! This is the day the Lord has made. Yesterday is gone. Last night before you slept, you gave your worries to the Lord and, hopefully, you trusted Him to work out all your troubles. Today, God gives you a fresh start, an opportunity to put aside those old, stale worries and look to the future with hope.

Psalm 118 is King David's prayer of praise. He said, "I cried to the Lord in my trouble, and He answered me and put me in a good place" (verse 5 NLV). His prayer is a testament to God's faithfulness, power, and strength. David recalled some of the ways the Lord saved him from trouble. He encouraged others to praise God too: "Let Israel say, 'His loving-kindness lasts forever.' Let the house of Aaron say, 'His loving-kindness lasts forever.' Let those who fear the Lord say, 'His loving-kindness lasts forever'" (verses 2–4 NLV).

Praise is a great way to replace worrisome thoughts with good thoughts. Dwelling on God's faithfulness will help make you strong. Embrace this new day! Instead of beginning it with worries, set your thoughts on God. Think of how He has been faithful to you and praise Him.

Pray:

Good morning, Lord. Thank You for this new day. I praise You for the many ways You have been faithful to me. Walk with me today. Remind me to keep my thoughts centered on You and Your goodness as I move forward with hope.

THE GOD WHO REMEMBERS

Read 1 Samuel 1:1–20

Key Verses:

Hannah was very troubled. She prayed to the Lord and cried with sorrow. Then she. . . said, "O Lord of All, be sure to look on the trouble of Your woman servant, and remember me. Do not forget Your woman servant."

1 Samuel 1:10–11 NLV

Understand:

- Have you poured out your troubles to God in prayer?
- Do you trust that God hears you when you pray?

Apply:

Hannah was one of Elkanah's two wives. His other wife, Peninnah, had children, Hannah did not, and Peninnah never let her forget it. She did her best to hurt Hannah by constantly reminding her that she wasn't a mom. This made Hannah so sad she wasn't even able to eat. What did Hannah do? She took her problem to the Lord in prayer. "O Lord of All, be sure to look on the trouble of Your woman servant, and remember me." Hannah prayed silently, pouring out all her troubles to God.

Hannah is a good example of what to do with our worries. When our hearts are troubled, we should pour them out to the Lord. When Hannah said, "Lord, remember me!" it wasn't because she thought God had forgotten her. It was a plea for Him to relieve her suffering, a fervent and hopeful prayer.

God never forgets us. It's just that His timing isn't always congruent with ours and His answers are often beyond our understanding. Make prayer a key element in relieving your worries. Hannah trusted God to work out her troubles, and so can you.

Pray:

O Lord, You are the God who remembers!
My spirit is troubled today, but I have faith
that You understand my hurt and worries.
I believe that in Your own time You will relieve
my suffering. Please comfort me now as I wait.

A PRAYER MODEL

Read Matthew 6:5–13

Key Verse:

"When you pray, do not say the same thing over and over again making long prayers like the people who do not know God. They think they are heard because their prayers are long."
MATTHEW 6:7 NLV

Understand:

- Do you ever find it hard to pray?
- Does anything stop you from talking with God as a friend?

Jesus was teaching about prayer in today's scripture reading. The passage includes a familiar prayer that you've likely heard or prayed many times, the Lord's Prayer: "Our Father which art in heaven. . ." (verse 9 KJV). It is a prayer we often recite without thinking about its words, but we need to think about them because they model a way to form our own prayers. Let's look at Matthew 6:9–13 and build a prayer.

- Verses 9 and 10: Begin by praising God. Ask Him to answer your prayer according to His will.

- Verse 11: Next, tell God what you need.
- Verse 12: Ask God to forgive your sins and to help you forgive those who have wronged you.
- Verse 13: Ask God to lead you away from Satan's traps. End your prayer by putting all your faith and trust in God's mighty power.

When you aren't sure how to pray, use Jesus' model in the Lord's Prayer. Prayer isn't reciting the same words over and over or saying everything perfectly. It's simply talking with God and speaking to Him as if you are talking with your best friend—because you are!

Pray:

Dear God, I praise You. Meet my needs today according to Your will. Forgive me for my sins, and help me to forgive those who sin against me. Keep me away from doing wrong. I trust in You and Your mighty power.

POSITIVE THOUGHTS

Read Philippians 4:4–8

Key Verse:

If there is anything good and worth giving thanks for, think about these things.

PHILIPPIANS 4:8 NLV

Understand:

- Why does positive thinking help when you worry?
- How did Paul stay positive while suffering in prison?

Apply:

The apostle Paul was in prison when he wrote to the Christian church in Philippi. Paul loved the people in this church, and they loved him. Although Paul was suffering greatly for preaching about Jesus, he encouraged his friends not to worry but to pray, and to be joyful because they belonged to the Lord. Paul reminded them that they would find peace beyond their understanding by giving God thanks and asking Him to meet their needs. Paul told them to keep their minds on what they had to be thankful for—"whatever is true, whatever is respected, whatever is right, whatever is pure, whatever can be loved, and whatever is well thought of" (Philippians 4:8 NLV).

Positive thoughts, along with prayer and keeping your mind and heart fixed on Jesus, are key to releasing your worries. This six-day written exercise can help you begin to think positively:

- Day 1: Jot down thoughts about God you believe to be true.
- Day 2: List some people and ideologies you respect.
- Day 3: Write down three to five things you firmly believe are right and pleasing to God.
- Day 4: Define what purity means to you.
- Day 5: Make a list of who and what you love.
- Day 6: Reread what you've written and thank God for His many blessings.

You might consider also keeping a daily journal of positive thoughts and prayers.

Pray:

Heavenly Father, remind me to set my thoughts on the many ways You bless me.

WHO IS SATAN?

Read Ezekiel 28:6–19

Key Verse:

"All who know you are appalled at your fate; you are an example of horror; you are destroyed forever."
EZEKIEL 28:19 TLB

Understand:

- Who was God speaking about in Ezekiel 28?
- What was Satan before God cast him out of heaven?
- What evidence do we have that Satan is active in the world today?

Apply:

Ezekiel 28 provides Satan's backstory and hints at his ultimate demise. Satan was once a mighty guardian angel in heaven, appointed by God and trusted by Him. But all the wisdom and riches God gave Satan went to his head. Pride made him think he was as powerful as God, and he used for his own gain everything God had given him. This made God very angry. He cast Satan out of heaven and called him "an example of horror." God vowed to destroy him forever.

We first meet Satan in the book of Genesis as the serpent who convinced Adam and Eve to sin. We see him in the Gospels (Matthew, Mark, Luke, and John) as he unsuccessfully tried to tempt Jesus. Throughout the Bible we find people giving in to Satan's temptations and suffering because of it. Then in the book of Revelation, God does what He promised and destroys Satan forever.

Satan is the source of everything evil, everything that leads us to worry and fear, and that is why we need to cast God's enemy out of our lives, like God cast him out of heaven.

Pray:

Lord God, help me to recognize Satan in my midst. Through Your Holy Spirit, caution me to turn away from him and toward You. Strengthen me to resist temptation and to trust that You will deliver me from evil.

THE ENEMY BRINGS SUFFERING

Read 1 Peter 5:6–11

Key Verse:

Stand against him and be strong in your faith. Remember, other Christians over all the world are suffering the same as you are.

1 Peter 5:9 NLV

Understand:

- Is all suffering caused by Satan?
- How can we endure our suffering?
- Does worry exacerbate our troubles?

Today's scripture reading encourages us to stand strong in faith so we can stand up to Satan. It reminds us that Christians all over the world suffer because of his evil—in other words, you are not alone. There is no one on earth who can escape evil, just as there is no one who can resist God's power. Peter told us to give our worries to God and then trust that in His time He will relieve our suffering. "Keep awake!" Peter said. "The devil is working against you" (1 Peter 5:8 NLV).

We can resist Satan by reading God's Word, knowing what pleases Him, and then doing our best to obey. We avoid a lot of worry and suffering by not falling for Satan's tricks. However, because everyone has free will, we can be victims of the bad choices others make. Their decisions can result in our suffering. When that happens, instead of blaming God, blame Satan, the enemy, the one who is the source of every sin and its aftermath.

God loves you. He gives you strength to resist temptation and also to endure its consequences. God has power over all things. When you put your trust in Him, God will bring you through your troubles so you can share in His shining-greatness forever.

Dear God, evil and suffering are a part of life, but I don't need to add worry and fear. You will lift me up from my troubles. Your goodness and love bring me peace.

FAITH OVER FEAR

Read Deuteronomy 31:1-8

Key Verse:

"The Lord is the One Who goes before you. He will be with you. He will be faithful to you and will not leave you alone. Do not be afraid or troubled."
DEUTERONOMY 31:8 NLV

Understand:

- How do you handle fear?
- What gives you strength?

Apply:

Moses is a good example of someone whom God led from fear to faith. When God told Moses to stand up to Egypt's powerful pharaoh and rescue the Israelites from slavery, Moses begged God to send someone else. But God said, "Go!" God had appointed Moses to lead the Israelites out of Egypt and to the land God promised them. The journey was years long and hard, and there was plenty of suffering. But with each step, each mile, each year, Moses grew stronger in faith.

In Deuteronomy 31:1–8, the Israelites were about to cross into the Promised Land, but they found it already occupied. The Israelites would have to fight for their land, and with a new leader, Joshua. Obviously, they were afraid. Moses told them, "Be strong and have strength of heart. Do not be afraid or shake with fear because of them. For the Lord your God is the One Who goes with you. He will be faithful to you. He will not leave you alone" (verse 6 NLV). Moses was certain God would lead them and everything would be okay.

Faith overcomes fear. Satan loves making us think we are weak, but God says we are strong. Ask Him today to strengthen you and build up your faith, as He did Moses'.

Pray:

Almighty God, sometimes fear overcomes me. It makes me weak, and instead of standing against it, I feel like running away. With You protecting me, I won't be afraid. Please give me a strong faith like Moses'. Lead me, Lord, and I will follow.

WISDOM OVER WORRY

Read 1 Kings 3:4–12

Key Verse:

"I will do what you have asked. I will give you a wise and discerning heart, so that there will never have been anyone like you, nor will there ever be."
1 Kings 3:12 NIV

Understand:

- What does *wisdom* mean to you?
- If you could ask God for anything at all, what would you ask for?

Apply:

Solomon was young when his father, King David, died. His exact age isn't known, but Bible scholars estimate he might have been around twenty or younger. Imagine becoming a king at that age. Add to it the fact that you are ruling over God's people, the great nation of Israel. Solomon was worried and probably afraid.

The young king needed God's help. He offered a thousand burnt offerings seeking God's favor, and then God appeared to Solomon in a dream. "Ask for whatever you want," God said. Solomon could have asked for power, for victory over Israel's enemies, for riches, or for anything else, but instead he asked for wisdom. Even at this young age, Solomon understood that wisdom would help him discern right from wrong and make wise decisions. Wisdom was the one thing he needed to solve all his problems in a way that pleased God. Solomon received from God a gift of wisdom so great that Solomon is known as the wisest person who ever lived.

You can read Solomon's thoughts in the book of Proverbs. But, better yet, pray and ask God to give you wisdom over worry, to help you discern right from wrong and make wise choices. The more you read and think about God's Word, the wiser you will become.

Pray:

God, please give me wisdom to overcome the problems I face today. Teach me to make decisions that are wise, right, and pleasing to You.

THE ONE AND ONLY GOD

Read Joshua 24:4–18

Key Verse:

The people answered, "May it never be that we turn away from the Lord and serve other gods."
JOSHUA 24:16 NLV

Understand:

- Does your family serve the one true God?
- False gods can be things like our phones, money, work, and even relationships. Can you name three more?

Apply:

"Thou shalt have no other gods before me" (Exodus 20:3 KJV). This was the first of God's Ten Commandments, and yet, while Moses was up on Mount Sinai receiving the commandments from God, the Israelites were so worried that God had abandoned them that they built a statue of a golden calf and worshipped it as their god.

As you read today's scripture passage, you find the Israelites' leader, Joshua, speaking to them as they settle into the Promised Land. He reminded them that while traveling from Egypt, some had given up on God and turned to worshipping false gods. Knowing they had free will, Joshua told them they could choose which god to serve, but he and his family would serve the one true God.

The Israelites vowed never to serve other gods, but still, worry and fear caused some to abandon God and replace Him with other things. This has been true throughout history and even today when there are more distractions than ever.

Satan is always tempting us with false gods. A false god is anything that becomes more important to you than your heavenly Father. When you put God first above everything else, His power gives you confidence to face your troubles and make good choices. Ponder that today. What place does God have in your life?

Pray:

Lord, help me to recognize the false gods that want to take Your place in my heart. By putting You first, I know that Your power working through me will help me to become confident, wise, and unafraid.

THE POWER OF PRAYER

Read Jonah 2

Key Verse:

*"While I was losing all my strength,
I remembered the Lord. And my prayer
came to You, into Your holy house."*
JONAH 2:7 NLV

Understand:

- Do you find it difficult to give God control of your life?
- Have you ever felt afraid to go where God is leading you?

Apply:

Jonah disobeyed. God commanded him to go to Nineveh and tell its people to change their evil ways. These people were enemies of the Israelites, and Jonah refused to go. Instead, he ran. If you read the entire story of Jonah, you will learn that he boarded a ship, was thrown overboard, and, as he sank to the bottom of the angry sea, was swallowed by a big fish. After Jonah spent three days praying inside the fish's belly, God made it spit Jonah out onto dry land.

When overcome by worry and fear, we sometimes

run from God instead of to Him. It's another way Satan gets in the way of our relationship with the Lord. Like Jonah, we become so preoccupied with worry or fear that we forget how powerful God is. When Jonah realized he was losing all his strength, he (finally) remembered God and prayed.

There is power in our prayers. When we prioritize prayer over worry, we strengthen our relationship with God. Romans 8:28 (NLV) says, "We know that God makes all things work together for the good of those who love Him and are chosen to be a part of His plan." When we pray and relinquish our control to God, we allow Him to work out our problems. He hears us, and He says, "Yes, I will help you."

Pray:

Dear God, whenever I begin to worry, remind me to run to You right away, to pray, to give You control over my situation, and to trust that You will work everything out for good.

THE POWER OF PERSISTENCE

Read 1 Kings 18:41–45

Key Verse:

And he said to his servant, "Go up now and look toward the sea." So he went up and looked and said, "There is nothing." Seven times Elijah said, "Go again."
1 Kings 18:43 NLV

Understand:

- Do you trust that God responds to every prayer?
- Do you wait patiently for God to answer?

Apply:

God told the prophet Elijah that He would punish the people with a long drought for worshipping false gods. Three years into the drought, God sent Elijah to King Ahab to say He was going to make it rain. Elijah delivered the message to the king, and then Elijah went to Mount Carmel to pray. Elijah said to his servant, "Go up now and look toward the sea." So the servant went up, looked for rain clouds, and said, "There is nothing." Elijah prayed again for rain. Six times he prayed. Six times he sent his servant to look for rain, and the servant saw nothing. We don't know how much time passed between each prayer. Elijah could have given up, but he didn't. The seventh time he prayed, his servant saw a small cloud. "Go tell King Ahab," Elijah said. Soon the sky became black with clouds and there was much rain.

Elijah's story is an example of persistence in prayer. He prayed with faith, trusting that God would do exactly what He said. Elijah prayed without ceasing, knowing that God hadn't given up on him—so he wasn't going to give up on God.

Do you pray with faith and persistence too?

Pray:

Heavenly Father, I haven't always prayed persistently. I just assumed that You had said no to my prayer. Teach me to trust that You will answer and to continue to ask until the Holy Spirit leads me elsewhere.

OUR MERCIFUL GOD

Read Ephesians 2:1–8

Key Verses:

But because of his great love for us, God,
who is rich in mercy, made us alive with Christ
even when we were dead in transgressions–
it is by grace you have been saved.
Ephesians 2:4–5 niv

Understand:

- Why do you think God is merciful?
- Has God forgiven all your sins?

Apply:

Some people believe that God will never forgive them for their sins. Maybe in their youth they lived in ways that were unrestrained, immoral, rebellious, or even illegal. They might have hurt people along the way. As they look back at what they have done, they are ashamed and ask themselves, *Why did I do that? How can I ever be forgiven?*

In today's scripture passage, Paul reminded his Christian friends that God is rich in mercy. Even though we were spiritually dead before, when we accepted Jesus Christ as our Lord and Savior, our past transgressions were all wiped away. Thanks to

God's mercy—loving-kindness—and His gift of salvation through Jesus, we can hold our heads high, free from shame.

If you are worried that God hasn't forgiven your past sins, remember that you were set free the minute you asked Jesus to come into your heart. You can't do anything to earn God's mercy and forgiveness. They are His gift to you—not just one day at a time, but forever. How can you thank Him? By living your life as best you can and helping others. That is how God planned for all of us to spend our lives.

Pray:

Dear God, I have done things in my life that I'm ashamed of, but I know that because You are merciful, You have forgiven me. Through my trust in Jesus, all my sins are washed away. Help me to learn from my past transgressions and to move forward unashamed.

THE POWER OF FORGIVENESS

Read Colossians 3:12–15

Key Verse:

Try to understand other people. Forgive each other. If you have something against someone, forgive him. That is the way the Lord forgave you.

COLOSSIANS 3:13 NLV

Understand:

- Do you believe there are conditions required to forgive someone?
- Does God forgive us unconditionally?

Apply:

When wounds cut deep and fail to heal, all we feel is the pain. Learning to forgive despite the pain requires all the characteristics outlined in Colossians 3:12–15. The first is loving-pity, or compassion. Sometimes this means having pity on those who don't know God and choose to do wrong. Next is kindness. In the Gospels, we see many examples of Jesus showing kindness to those who don't deserve it. Humility is another key to forgiveness; pride often gets in the way of our ability to forgive. Patience is required too, patience with ourselves as we heal from our hurts and are ready to forgive. Add to all these things love—loving others the way God loves us.

The takeaway from Colossians 3:12–15 is that God wants us to forgive each other the way He forgives us, fully, completely, and with no strings attached. There is power in forgiveness because it frees us from the burden of carrying around anger and hurt. Forgiveness doesn't mean forgetting or saying that what someone did was okay. It simply means we choose to forgive them anyway. Forgiveness is a way of sharing God's love with others even when they don't deserve it.

Pray:

Father, forgive me for my unforgiveness. I've sometimes been unwilling to let go of anger, resentment, and bitterness. But, to please You and for my own good, I know that I must. Please help me to be forgiving of those who hurt me or make me angry. Free me from the burden of an unforgiving heart.

THE POWER OF HOPE

Read Lamentations 3:1-25

Key Verses:

It is because of the Lord's loving-kindness that we are not destroyed for His loving-pity never ends. It is new every morning. He is so very faithful.

LAMENTATIONS 3:22–23 NLV

Understand:

- Thinking about the future, what are you most worried about losing?
- Even if you lost everything, would you still trust in God's faithfulness?

In Lamentations 3, the prophet Jeremiah described the aftermath of Babylon's destruction of Jerusalem. God allowed it to be destroyed because its people had rejected His warning, through Jeremiah, that Jerusalem would be attacked and overtaken. Some Bible scholars believe that Jeremiah's first-person account in Lamentations is as if the city and its citizens were speaking.

After Jerusalem had been destroyed, its people, the Jews, were held captive in Babylonia. Their hope of returning home was gone. But Jeremiah knew that help was coming. He had seen it before—God picking up the pieces, putting them together again, and restoring what was broken or torn down. The Lord is merciful and wonderfully good to those who don't lose hope but wait for Him.

Today, we see images of destruction caused by wars around the world. We see people suffering as the Jews had when Babylon's army invaded their city. Throughout history, wars and other tragedies have destroyed people and their property, but God always rebuilds when people put their hope in Him.

Maybe you are worried about losing something, or maybe you are mourning a loss. Pray. Don't ever lose hope. As long as you are alive, God will be faithful. When you put your hope in Him, He will restore you.

Pray:

Lord God, I worry about losing people I love and things I need. I have no control over the future, but I do have control over my worries and fears. Help me never to lose hope in Your faithfulness. You are wonderfully good to me.

THE POWER OF JOY

Read Nehemiah 8:1–12

Key Verse:

And all the people went away to eat and drink, to share what they had, and to show their joy. They understood the words which had been made known to them.

Nehemiah 8:12 NLV

Understand:

- What about God brings you joy?
- Can you think of a time when God changed your worries or sadness to joy?

Apply:

God was faithful. The people had waited with hope for Jerusalem to be rebuilt so they could return home, and finally, the day had come. The book of Nehemiah tells what happened next. Ezra stood up before the people and began reading from the scriptures. He read all day. The crowd listened quietly, and helpers walked among the people answering questions so they could better understand what Ezra read. It had been a long time since they had heard the scriptures, and some people wept when they heard and understood the Word of God. "Don't weep," Ezra told them. "This is a special day to honor the Lord. The joy of the Lord is your strength." So the people celebrated. They ate, drank, and shared with each other. They had a party! All their past worries and sadness were washed away by their good and faithful God. Their hearts were filled with joy when they heard and understood His words.

If you feel sad or worried, reading in the Bible about God's strength, love, and power over all your troubles is enough to bring you joy. Celebrate His faithfulness today. He is the God who will never let you down.

Pray:

Your Word brings me joy, Lord. The more I read of Your faithfulness, love, and commitment to my happiness, the more I realize You are the source of my joy. Your blessings are never ending!

THE POWER OF PRAISE

Read Exodus 15:1–21

Key Verse:

"The LORD is my strength and my defense; he has become my salvation. He is my God, and I will praise him, my father's God, and I will exalt him."

EXODUS 15:2 NIV

Understand:

- Why should we praise God?
- How can we praise Him?
- How does praising God help us?

Apply:

Moses rescued the Israelites from slavery in Egypt. As he led them away, they were pursued by Pharaoh's army—warriors armed with bows and spears, riding in horse-drawn chariots. As the Israelites reached the Red Sea, they thought surely they were doomed. But God opened a path through the sea, allowing the Israelites to walk safely to the other side. Then the sea closed up, swallowing Pharaoh's army. Today's scripture passage is a song of praise the Israelites sang to the Lord.

God loves hearing His people praise Him. He expects it. When He rescues us from trouble, we should praise Him. When we experience something joyful or are in awe of the beauty surrounding us, we should react with praise. Even when things look dismal, we should praise God anyway because of His ability to change darkness to light. He can hurl our troubles into the sea, just as He did Pharaoh's army.

There is power in praise. It is a great tool to help calm our worries and fears. Praising God lifts us up and brings us into closer fellowship with Him. Praise God today! Thank Him for His goodness and exalt His mighty power.

Pray:

Lord God, I praise You! I praise You for making a path through my troubles and for calming my fears. I praise You for protecting me, guiding me, and loving me. You are my strength and my salvation now and forever. O Lord God, I praise You!

READING THE PSALMS

Read Psalm 23

Key Verse:

Yes, even if I walk through the valley of the shadow of death, I will not be afraid of anything, because You are with me.

Psalm 23:4 NLV

Understand:

- Think of a time when God gave you strength when you needed it.
- List three ways God provided for your needs today.
- How do you know that God is always with you?

Apply:

Most of the Psalms were written by King David. Psalm 23 is the most well known. David had a life of triumphs, trouble, and tragedy. As a boy, he bravely conquered the enormous Philistine soldier, Goliath. Later, David was pursued by a jealous king and lived in fear and hiding until the king's death. David eventually became king of Israel, made Jerusalem its capital, fought enemy armies, and celebrated many victories. He was a good king, but he had moral failures. David committed adultery, had a child out of wedlock, and arranged for the death of Bathsheba's husband. He also suffered through the death of a child and dealt with rebellious children. We can relate to David. He was a good man who sometimes fell into sin's traps. As we read through the Psalms, we see him confess his sins, weep, repent, pray, question God, praise Him, and through it all, build a strong, faithful relationship with God.

When you feel worried or afraid, reading the Psalms can help. Psalm 23:4 summarizes what David learned and what we should remember—we need not be afraid of anything, because God is always with us.

Pray:

Dear heavenly Father, David's life was similar to mine, filled with triumphs and tragedies. You guided him through his troubles and gave him strength. As I read the Psalms, Lord, help me to see the many ways You help, love, and provide for me. Through David's words, build up my faith.

A TREE BY THE RIVER

Read Jeremiah 17:7–8

Key Verse:

"But blessed is the one who trusts in the LORD, whose confidence is in him."
JEREMIAH 17:7 NIV

Understand:

- In today's passage, what made the tree grow big and strong?
- How would you rate your confidence in God's faithfulness?

Apply:

The Bible contains many comparisons that help us understand God's words. One is found in today's Bible reading. The person who trusts God is like a tree planted by a river. The tree stretches its roots toward the water, and the water helps it grow big and strong. Not even a long drought can destroy that tree, because the river sustains it. We are the tree and God is the river. God plants the seed of faith inside our hearts. He wants us to reach out to Him and discover that we can trust Him to sustain us. As we learn to trust, our faith grows stronger. We become like that tree, confident that with God's help nothing can destroy us.

In Jeremiah 17, we find another comparison. It describes someone who won't reach out in faith. It says, "That person will be like a bush in the wastelands; they will not see prosperity when it comes. They will dwell in the parched places of the desert, in a salt land where no one lives" (verse 6 NIV). We can imagine that person always worried and afraid, dreading tomorrow and what it might bring.

Those who trust with confidence have no worries. Even when trouble comes they aren't afraid; they know God will save them. So reach out to Him in faith and trust Him. He will strengthen you, and as your confidence in Him grows, your worries will decrease.

Pray:

God, make me like that tree by the river. Help me to become confident in Your faithfulness and assured that nothing—nothing at all—can take me down.

SUDDEN TROUBLE

Read Mark 4:35-41

Key Verse:

Jesus was in the back part of the boat sleeping on a pillow. They woke Him up, crying out, "Teacher, do You not care that we are about to die?"

MARK 4:38 NLV

Understand:

- What lessons can we learn from Mark 4:35–41?
- What is the first thing you would do today if you faced serious trouble?

Apply:

Imagine lying in bed late at night awake and worried as a storm rages outside. Rain pummels hard against the windows. A sudden flash of lightning followed by a deafening clap of thunder makes you duck under the covers. You hear wind rushing through the trees. Your husband lies peacefully beside you snoring and unaware. Do you let him sleep, or do you give him a good, hard shove and exclaim, "Wake up! Don't you know there's a bad storm?"

In Mark 4:35–41, Jesus and His disciples were

in the middle of a lake, in a small boat, with a storm raging around them. Waves crashed into the boat, and it started to fill with water. The disciples were terrified, and probably a little irritated because there, at the back of the boat, Jesus was sound asleep on a comfy pillow. "Wake up!" they shouted. "Don't You care we're about to die!" What little faith His disciples had. Didn't they know they had nothing to fear as long as Jesus was with them?

Mark 4:35–41 is a story to recall when trouble floods our lives. Jesus never sleeps nor is He unaware of what's going on. He is wide awake to all our circumstances, and when we remember that He is with us, we have nothing to fear. Jesus will calm the storm.

Pray:

Lord Jesus, when suddenly I face trouble, my first instinct is to panic. Teach me not to be afraid and to trust that You are with me and will save me.

REST AND PRAY

Read Luke 5:12-16

Key Verses:

Yet the news about him spread all the more, so that crowds of people came to hear him and to be healed of their sicknesses. But Jesus often withdrew to lonely places and prayed.

Luke 5:15–16 NIV

Understand:

- What did you learn about rest from Luke 5:12–16?
- Do you make time each day for quiet rest and prayer?
- Can you think of a quiet place during your day where you can take a short break to rest and pray?

Apply:

As news spread about Jesus' ability to work miracles and heal diseases, large crowds followed Him. The people were intrigued by His teaching. They wanted to hear more of what He had to say. Imagine, day after day, being followed by hundreds, even thousands, of people, talking with them, healing their illnesses and disabilities, and speaking about how

God wanted them to live. How tiring it must have been for Jesus. He needed to go someplace quiet where He could be alone, rest, and pray. "Jesus *often* withdrew to lonely places and prayed," Luke 5:16 says (emphasis added). Rest was a part of Jesus' routine.

We all need rest—to take a break from all the busyness and business that fills our days. Rest not only refreshes our bodies, but when we combine it with meditation and prayer, it refreshes our souls. Incorporating times during the day to be alone and pray helps calm our worries. It leads us into a closer relationship with our Lord.

Pray:

Dear Jesus, lead me to that quiet place where I can rest awhile with You. Talk with me there; calm my nerves; give strength to my soul so I can go about my day ready and refreshed.

OUR TRUSTWORTHY GOD

Read Numbers 23:1–20

Key Verse:

"God is not a man, that He should lie. He is not a son of man, that He should be sorry for what He has said. Has He said, and will He not do it? Has He spoken, and will He not keep His Word?"

NUMBERS 23:19 NLV

Understand:

- What does *trust* mean to you?
- Can you think of a time when God showed you He is trustworthy?

Apply:

In Numbers 23, the Israelites, while traveling to the Promised Land, approached the land of Moab. Its king, Balak, worried about an invasion. He knew the Israelites were more powerful than his army. So the king called on Balaam to put a curse on the Israelites. Balaam had knowledge of God and was considered by some to be a prophet of God, but he was also soothsayer—a pagan foreteller of the future. Balaam told the king to build seven altars and burn seven bulls and rams as a sacrifice. Then

Balaam went off by himself to see if God would speak to him. Regardless of Balaam's true motives, God used him to convey a message to Balak. God said He would not allow Balaam to curse the Israelites. Instead, He would bless them. Nothing more needed to be said. God had spoken.

In our key verse today, Balaam spoke of the character of God: He will not lie. He is not sorry for what He says. He does exactly what He says, and He keeps His promises.

Our all-powerful God is trustworthy. His words are set in stone forever. God doesn't change. When trouble and worries invade our hearts, we can trust in His goodness and love. We can trust God to help us.

Pray:

Dear heavenly Father, please help me to build up my trust in You so it is solid and unwavering.

THE CONDITION OF OUR FAITH

Read Revelation 3:14–22

Key Verse:

"See! I stand at the door and knock. If anyone hears My voice and opens the door, I will come in to him and we will eat together."

REVELATION 3:20 NLV

Understand:

- Would you say your love for the Lord is zealous, or is it lukewarm?
- Have you asked Jesus to come into your heart? Why or why not?

The book of Revelation is John's account of visions given him regarding the end times. In chapter 3, Jesus instructed John to write to the church in Laodicea. Some of the early Christian churches had allowed wealth to make their faithfulness lukewarm. Other churches had become morally corrupt. Churches that remained faithful were often persecuted and harassed for their strong commitment to Christ. Jesus warned the churches that the end times were coming, and they needed to shape up and follow Him.

Revelation 3:20 is a familiar verse: "See! I stand at the door and knock. If anyone hears My voice and opens the door, I will come in." It isn't only Christ's message to the early churches. It is also His message to us. He knocks on the doors to our hearts, wanting to come in. Jesus desires a relationship with us that isn't lukewarm, but one in which we want to be with Him all the time and live to please Him. In today's reading, He urged the churches to examine the condition of their faith. This is something all of us should do—examine our spiritual condition and ask ourselves, *Is my faith passionate, or is it just lukewarm?*

Pray:

Lord, I want to please You. Forgive me for times when life gets in the way and my faith becomes lukewarm. Thank You for loving me anyway and for reminding me that You want to come first in my life.

OUR GUIDEBOOK

Read Hebrews 4:12–16

Key Verse:

Let us go with complete trust to the throne of God. We will receive His loving-kindness and have His loving-favor to help us whenever we need it.

Hebrews 4:16 NLV

Understand:

- How often do you read the Bible?
- As you read the Bible, do you stop and think about its words?
- Have you explored different versions of the Bible and found one you prefer?

Apply:

Today's scripture reading speaks of several things—(1) the power of God's Word, (2) the importance of following the example Christ set for us, and (3) prayer. Let's break them down.

First, when we meditate on God's Word, it teaches us what God wants from us. It convicts us of where we can improve and encourages us to confess our sins to God. These things—learning how to please Him, recognizing our sins, and wanting to do better—bring us into a closer relationship with Him.

Second, Hebrews 4:14 (NLV) refers to Jesus as our "great Religious Leader." The Gospels are where we study Jesus' character. We please God when we model our behavior after His Son. We can learn from Jesus how to get along with others and what to do with emotions that are negative or cause us worry and pain.

Finally, Hebrews 4:16 encourages us to pray with confidence and not be afraid to approach God with our requests and our confessions. It assures us of His loving-kindness and willingness to help with all our situations.

The Bible is our guide for living. As we study its words and apply them, our faith grows stronger, and our lives become less stressful.

Pray:

Dear God, guide me through Your Word and open my eyes to how it applies specifically to my life. As I read, help me to grow in faith and lead me into a closer relationship with You.

IS IT TIME TO MOVE ON?

Read Isaiah 43:2–3, 18–19

Key Verse:

"Do not remember the things that have happened before. Do not think about the things of the past."

Isaiah 43:18 NLV

Understand:

- Is something from the past keeping you from moving on?
- Have situations from the past caused you to worry about the future?

Apply:

The Israelites suffered much after being rescued from slavery in Egypt. They wandered through the desert for forty years before finally entering the Promised Land. They fought enemies, experienced hunger, became discouraged, even worshipped a false god. Still, God never left them, nor did He change the good plans He had for them. Whatever they encountered, God promised to protect them. We can imagine that they often thought about all the trouble they had experienced and the obstacles that got in their way. Maybe those thoughts filled their minds and made them afraid and reluctant to move on.

Today's key verse is God telling the Israelites not to dwell on the past. God had a new plan for them. It was already happening. God asked if they didn't see it. He was making a path for them through the wilderness and rivers of water in the desert.

When we dwell on negative things from the past, it leads us to worry about the future. God says, "Do not remember the things that have happened before. Do not think about the things of the past." We can move on with faith and confidence that God will make a way for us just as He did for the Israelites. His plans for us are good.

Pray:

Father, You know what I've been through,
and You understand why I'm reluctant
to let go of my worries and move on.
Please give me courage to put the past
behind me and to move forward with faith.

THE ARMOR OF GOD

Read Ephesians 6:10–17

Key Verse:

So stand up and do not be moved.
EPHESIANS 6:14 NLV

Understand:

- What do you think it means to stand against, or resist, the devil?
- Thinking about the armor of God, are there parts you need God's help to strengthen?

Apply:

In the Bible, James said, "Stand against the devil and he will run away from you" (James 4:7 NLV). In today's reading, Paul added what we need to stand up to Satan and his demons. Paul used the analogy of armor comprised of pieces:

- Belt of truth—wisdom to discern what is right according to God
- Breastplate of righteousness—believing we are God's children and He will fight for us
- Shoes of peace—willingness to

stand up for and tell others the gospel of Christ

- Shield of faith—unwavering belief in God's mighty power
- Helmet of salvation—trusting that through Christ our sins are forever forgiven
- Sword of the Spirit—the Bible, the Word of God

All these things when combined protect us from evil.

Christians have different views of what it means to resist Satan. Some believe it means engaging in a fight against him. Others believe it means standing tall in faith and trust and allowing God's mighty power to make Satan flee. Maybe it's a combination of both. Whatever we believe, God gives us the strength to resist. Don't let worry, fear, and sin destroy your ability to stand strong. Put on the armor of God and stand!

Pray:

Lord God, You are my strength and my shield.
When I put all my faith and trust in You,
I needn't fear Satan's tricks. With Your power
working through me, I have everything
I need to stand firm and resist his evil ways.
Thank You, Lord, for protecting me.

BIG PROBLEMS

Read 1 Samuel 17

Key Verse:

Then David said to the Philistine, "You come to me with a sword and spears. But I come to you in the name of the Lord of All, the God of the armies of Israel, Whom you have stood against."

1 Samuel 17:45 NLV

Understand:

- What is the biggest problem you have ever faced?
- Would you say you faced that big problem bravely or with worry and fear?
- Name three tools God gives us to stand up to trouble.

Apply:

King Saul and his soldiers were afraid of the giant Philistine soldier, Goliath. Some scholars estimate that Goliath was almost ten feet tall. He was mean and menacing and dressed from head to foot in sturdy armor. Young David wasn't afraid, though. He bravely agreed to fight Goliath. Although Saul encouraged David to wear armor, David refused. With only a stick, five smooth stones, and his slingshot, David prepared to fight. The giant ambled toward David. He stood tall talking against God and making fun of the shepherd boy. But David didn't back down. "The battle is the Lord's," David said, "and He will give you into our hands" (1 Samuel 17:47 NLV). Then David, the shepherd boy, aimed his slingshot at Goliath's forehead. With just one stone, David knocked the giant down—forever!

When we face big problems, we can draw courage from David's story. If we stand up to trouble and entrust the battle to God, He will help us overpower whatever gets in our way. Its size doesn't matter. Nothing is too big or too powerful for our almighty God.

Pray:

Heavenly Father, the battle against evil belongs to You. Give me courage and strength to face big problems head-on, knowing that You go before me and You will fight for me.

I WILL RISE

Read Micah 7:2–8

Key Verse:

Do not have joy over me, you who hate me. When I fall, I will rise. Even though I am in darkness, the Lord will be my light.

MICAH 7:8 NLV

Understand:

- Think of a time when someone hurt or betrayed you.
- How did you handle the hurt or broken trust?
- What can help you rise above feelings of mistrust?

Apply:

Have you been betrayed? Has broken trust made you think there aren't any good people left in the world? Maybe you worry about being betrayed again.

Micah's words in today's reading still apply. People turn against each other. Evil lies in wait ready to do harm, and corrupt leaders plan against people instead of helping them. Micah said the best of them is like a thistle. The most honest are like a thornbush. He went on, warning us not to trust even those closest to us.

Yes, there is evil in the world, and yes, sometimes even those closest betray us. But when we are hurt or betrayed, God will help us pick up the pieces; and then, with confidence, we will rise. There are trustworthy people in the world modeling their lives after Christ. God will help us discern who they are. When someone knocks us down, our heavenly Father will help and will lead us to those who will pick us up. God is always trustworthy. We can't allow the hurt someone caused to stop us from believing in goodness. Rise above it. Let the Lord heal your hurt and teach you to trust again.

Pray:

Dear God, someone has hurt me deeply. It has made me lose trust in people. Please help me to rise above the pain. Teach me to discern who is trustworthy and help me to trust again.

FAITHFUL FAMILY AND FRIENDS

Read Exodus 17:1–13

Key Verse:

Moses' hands became tired. So they took a stone and put it under him, and he sat on it. Then Aaron and Hur held up his hands, one on each side. His hands did not move until the sun went down.

Exodus 17:12 NLV

Understand:

- Who are your most trusted friends, and why do you trust them?
- Can you think of times you felt worried or afraid and a family member "held up your hands"?

Apply:

If you study Moses in the Bible, you will see how much he grew in confidence and faith while leading the Israelites out of Egypt to the Promised Land. The people didn't always have faith in God or in Moses, and their complaining caused Moses trouble. He did have people who supported him, though.

In today's reading, we see Moses growing weary of holding up the staff of God during a battle with the Amalekites. As long as Moses raised the stick, the Israelites won; if he put it down, the enemy took the lead. Moses' brother, Aaron, and his nephew, Hur, saw that Moses needed help, so they rushed in. They brought a stone for Moses to sit on, and they held up his hands. With the Lord and others on his side, Moses didn't have to worry. He held up the stick, and his people won the battle.

Faithful, God-loving family members and friends notice when someone is worried, is afraid, or needs help. They come to the aid of others and "hold up their hands." With God and those you trust on your side, you can worry less, assured you are never alone.

Pray:

Dear God, make me someone who notices the needs of others. Open my eyes to family members and friends who could use some support, and show me how I can help.

EVEN IF HE DOES NOT

Read Daniel 3:8–30

Key Verse:

"But even if He does not, we want you to know, O king, that we will not serve your gods or worship the object of gold that you have set up."
Daniel 3:18 NLV

Understand:

- If you were Shadrach, Meshach, or Abed-nego, would you have denied God?
- How can you build a faith so strong that nothing could make you turn from Him?

King Nebuchadnezzar ordered that his subjects get on their knees and worship his gold statue. Death was the penalty, to be thrown into a fiery furnace. Shadrach, Meshach, and Abed-nego refused to obey. "And what god is able to save you?" asked the king. The men answered, "Our God Whom we serve is able to save us" (Daniel 3:15, 17 NLV). Their loyalty to God was sure, so sure that they added, "But even if He does not, we want you to know, O king, that we will not serve your gods or worship the object of gold" (verse 18 NLV). These men were human, after all, and surely they were concerned that God's plan might not be to save them from the fire; but still, they left the outcome to Him.

Imagine a faith so strong that even facing death, you could surrender the outcome to God, a faith so strong that even if someone threatened to kill you if you didn't deny God, you would say, "No!" In the Bible, we read of those who said no and lost their lives and others who said no and lived. A faith that strong comes from our heavenly Father who loves us. Not even death separates us from His love.

Pray:

Father, in every frightening situation I face, let my faith in You overcome my fear. I want a faith so strong that nothing on earth could make me deny You.

SPEAK UP

Read Romans 8:33–39

Key Verse:

For I know that nothing can keep us from the love of God. Death cannot! Life cannot! Angels cannot! Leaders cannot! Any other power cannot! Hard things now or in the future cannot!

ROMANS 8:38 NLV

Understand:

- Do you worry about being rejected for expressing your faith in God?
- Have you ever been made fun of for your faith?
- How willing are you to talk about Jesus in the presence of nonbelievers?

Apply:

Some Christians worry they will be rejected or ridiculed if they speak about Jesus and stand up for their faith. From the days when Jesus walked on earth until now, those who believe in Him have been rejected and made fun of by nonbelievers. Early Christians were imprisoned, tortured, and put to death for sharing the gospel of Christ. Still, they kept speaking about Him and His loving gift of salvation.

Romans 8:33–39 reminds us that God knows those who are right with Him. He loves those who love Him, and nothing can separate them from His love. We have power over our fear of being rejected and ridiculed for our faith. Satan puts that fear in us. The very essence of faith is being willing to put the Lord above our feelings. True faith is being willing to speak freely about God without fearing the rejection of nonbelievers. They are the ones who need most to hear about Jesus. When we speak of our love for Christ and His love for us, our words may be what God uses to open the door for Him to enter into their hearts.

Pray:

Lord Jesus, may I never be reluctant to speak of Your goodness and love in the presence of nonbelievers. I can't know when the time is right for them to hear of Your gift of salvation, but may my words resonate with them and lead them to welcome You into their hearts.

LORD, I SIMPLY ASK. . .

Read 1 Chronicles 4:9–10

Key Verse:

"Oh, that you would wonderfully bless me and help me in my work; please be with me in all that I do, and keep me from all evil and disaster!" And God granted him his request.
1 Chronicles 4:10 TLB

Understand:

- Do you think God cares about the length of our prayers?
- Is a short, simple prayer as effective as one that is repeated over and over or has many words?

Apply:

Jesus said in Matthew 6:7 that we don't need to pray long prayers. Short prayers can be just as powerful and effective. Peter cried out in fear, "Lord, save me!" (Matthew 14:30 NLV). Moses interceded for his sister: "O God, heal her, I pray!" (Numbers 12:13 NLV). In Luke 18:13 (NLV), the tax collector said, "God, have pity on me! I am a sinner!"

Today's key verse is the prayer of a man named Jabez. The Bible says very little about Jabez except that he was an honorable man; yet, in the long ancestry list in 1 Chronicles 4, his prayer was important enough to be included along with his name. What can we learn from it? It is a model of a simple and direct prayer, short and not filled with flowery words or repetition. "Lord, bless me, help me, be with me, and keep me from evil. Amen."

It is wonderful to have conversations with God in prayer, worshipping and praising Him, telling Him our thoughts and worries, and so on, but it is perfectly fine to keep our prayers short. God already knows what we need; still, He wants us to bring our requests to Him. Tell God what you need today, and then trust that He will answer you.

Pray:

Dear Lord, please bless me, and answer my requests according to Your will. Today, I need. . .

WELL DONE!

Read Proverbs 31:10–31

Key Verse:

Give her the fruit of her hands,
and let her works praise her in the gates.
PROVERBS 31:31 NLV

Understand:

- What did you learn from reading Proverbs 31:10–31?
- How do you feel when your work isn't noticed or praised?
- Is it enough that God is pleased with your work?

Apply:

Did you see yourself in today's reading? Times have changed, but the role of wife and mother hasn't. Yes, we are liberated and more independent, but still, we care for our family's needs. We plan, schedule, cook, clean, do laundry, wipe tears, change diapers, fix what's broken. . .and we often do it while working a full-time job. Our everyday work stretches from dawn to well past dusk. Proverbs 31:10–31 praises women for the work they do. It encourages husbands and children to praise them too.

Do you ever feel like your work goes unnoticed? Some women take the absence of recognition as a sign they aren't doing enough, and that can lead to insecurity, worry, depression, and even self-loathing—all the emotions Satan loves. Even if you don't get the praise you deserve, God sees and He says, "Well done!" You are a godly woman, and your work is worthy of recognition and praise. Ephesians 6:5 tells us to work for others as if we are working for the Lord. Give yourself praise for all that you do, and find joy knowing that your hard work pleases your heavenly Father.

Pray:

O Lord, I'm weary of working so hard without recognition. I want praise from others. I want to know I'm appreciated. If that appreciation doesn't come, Lord, remind me that it is enough that You see and You are pleased by the work that I do.

TAMING OUR THOUGHTS

Read 2 Corinthians 10:1-6

Key Verse:

We break down every thought and proud thing that puts itself up against the wisdom of God. We take hold of every thought and make it obey Christ.
2 Corinthians 10:5 NLV

Understand:

- What do you think Paul meant when he said, "We do not fight like people of the world" (2 Corinthians 10:3 NLV)?
- What does it mean to break down every thought?
- What are some ways you can apply 2 Corinthians 10:5 to your everyday life?

Apply:

In 2 Corinthians 10:1–6, Paul reminded us that Christians fight evil differently than the rest of the world. We fight with the tools God gives us. Remember the armor of God—the belt of truth, the breastplate of righteousness, the shoes of peace, the shield of faith, the helmet of salvation, and the sword of the Spirit (Ephesians 6:10–17)? We have those tools to fight with; and, in today's key verse, Paul identified another tool, the ability to take hold of our thoughts and make them obey Christ.

How often do you think about your thoughts? They can lead us near to or away from God. Thoughts that are worrisome or self-deprecating or that contradict God's Word are those we need to tame. We do that by becoming more aware of what we are thinking and making a conscious effort to replace those thoughts with others. It takes practice, but with God's help anything is possible. To get started, reread Philippians 4:8 in your Bible. Write it down and put it where you will see it every day. Think about what is true, respected, right, pure, and loved.

Pray:

Dear God, guide me to be more aware of what I am thinking. Help me to take my thoughts captive and to change any that pull me away from You.

WORRY AND FEAR

Read Joshua 1:1-9

Key Verse:

"Have I not commanded you? Be strong and courageous. Do not be afraid; do not be discouraged, for the LORD your God will be with you wherever you go."

JOSHUA 1:9 NIV

Understand:

- What have you thought about most often today?
- What did you learn from today's reading about how to calm worry and fear?

Apply:

Moses had led the people to the edge of the Promised Land. Now he was dead, and Joshua was in charge of leading the people into their homeland. It required taking back the land from those who lived there, and we can imagine that Joshua was worried about his huge responsibility. Did you notice, as you read, that God told him three times to be strong and courageous? The third time, God added, "Do not be afraid; do not be discouraged."

Holocaust survivor and author Corrie ten Boom

once said, "Worry is a cycle of inefficient thoughts whirling around a center of fear."* Surely worrisome, frightening thoughts whirled around Joshua's mind that day. But God calmed his fear by reminding Joshua, "I will be with you; I will never leave you nor forsake you" (Joshua 1:5 NIV). He commanded Joshua to meditate on the Word of God night and day and do everything written in it. He said that would make Joshua prosperous and successful.

When worrisome thoughts whirl through your mind, remember that they come from fear. Try calming them with God's words to Joshua: "Have I not commanded you? Be strong and courageous. Do not be afraid; do not be discouraged, for [I] will be with you wherever you go." Everything you worry about, God has already worked out. You needn't be afraid.

Pray:

Dear God, thank You for calming my fears and for reminding me that You have all my concerns and worries under control.

* *Jesus Is Victor* (Revell Company, 1985).

WHO AM I?

Read Galatians 3:26–29

Key Verse:

For now we are all children of God through faith in Jesus Christ.
GALATIANS 3:26 TLB

Understand:

- How would you answer the question "Who am I?"
- How does being a child of God factor into your identity?

Apply:

Isn't it wonderful knowing that Jesus wraps His arms around us when we accept Him as our Lord and Savior? The Living Bible says in Galatians 3:27 that we are "enveloped by him." Instead of identifying merely as women who are Methodist or Baptist or Lutheran. . .faith in Jesus makes us, first and foremost, Christians—all the same in Christ—and through Him we are confirmed as children of God.

Who are you? You are a child of God. Ponder that for a moment. You are a daughter of the King of all kings, the Creator of the universe. God, your heavenly Father, created you, and He has always loved you with a love beyond any other you can imagine. His promises in the Bible belong to you. You are an heir to all He offers. Add to that Jesus, the one who makes it possible for you to live forever in heaven. He said, "I call you [friend], because I have told you everything I have heard from My Father" (John 15:15 NLV). Jesus will always be your most loyal and trustworthy best friend.

If you sometimes ask yourself, *Who am I?* and struggle with your sense of self-worth, remember that you are God's child. He values you, and He wants you to prosper. Ask Him today to transform you into the woman He wants you to be.

Pray:

Dear Father, thank You for reminding me that I am Your daughter. You love me, and I am of great worth to You. If I think poorly about myself, I want to remember that You made me beautiful and capable—and I am loved.

I AM REDEEMED!

Read Isaiah 64:4–8

Key Verse:

But now, O Lord, You are our Father.
We are the clay, and You are our pot maker.
All of us are the work of Your hand.
ISAIAH 64:8 NLV

Understand:

- In the Old Testament, what were the consequences of sin?
- How does sin factor into your identity?

Apply:

In the Old Testament, we find people worrying that their sins might never be forgiven. They knew sin led to death, and they felt afraid. God wanted His children to reject sin by obeying Him, but they were unable to keep themselves from falling into Satan's traps. "Will we be saved?" the people asked (Isaiah 64:5 NLV). They didn't know about God's great plan to send Jesus to lead them to forgiveness and eternal life.

Today, forgiveness for our sins is guaranteed when we accept Jesus as our Lord and Savior. We are redeemed—rescued from our sins, forgiven, and made right in our relationship with God. That opens our hearts to Him so He can mold us into our best selves. Isaiah 64:8 says we are like clay in God's hands. In the New Testament, 2 Corinthians 5:17 (NLV) tells us, "For if a man belongs to Christ, he is a new person. The old life is gone. New life has begun."

If you have asked Jesus into your heart, you are redeemed. Unlike those who lived in Old Testament days, you don't have to worry that sin leads to death. Despite your sins, you are forgiven and promised a place in heaven.

Pray:

Dear God, through Jesus I am redeemed; my old life is gone. Deliver me from guilt and shame for past transgressions and lead me to the new life You have planned for me.

I AM CHOSEN

Read 1 Peter 2:9–17

Key Verse:

But you are a chosen group of people. You are the King's religious leaders. You are a holy nation. You belong to God. He has done this for you so you can tell others how God has called you out of darkness into His great light.

1 PETER 2:9 NLV

Understand:

- What did you learn about yourself from reading 1 Peter 2:9–17?
- How does being a Christian factor into your identity?

God wants everyone to be saved and redeemed. He wants them to be part of His family. If you are a Christian, you are one of God's chosen people. You are not only His child but also His representative here on earth. Today's reading lists ways Christians honor God by representing Him:

- All Christians have a story of how they came to know God and were changed by Him. God wants them to share their story.

- Christians understand that their real home is in heaven. God placed them on earth for a purpose—to lead others to salvation and to serve Him by doing good.
- Around other people, even those they dislike, Christians talk and act in ways that please God. They model Christlike behavior.
- Christians obey their leaders and are respectful to everyone.
- Christians love each other, and they love and honor God.

So many things define who you are. Put at the top of your list "I am a Christian, a child of God, forgiven and redeemed. I am His representative here on earth." Remember these things, and your heavenly Father will lift you up from your worries and make you strong.

Pray:

Dear God, teach me not only to say, "I am a Christian," but in all my ways to reflect what it means to be one. Help me to represent You well here on earth.

I AM A CITIZEN OF HEAVEN

Read Philippians 3:10–21

Key Verse:

But we are citizens of heaven. Christ, the One Who saves from the punishment of sin, will be coming down from heaven again. We are waiting for Him to return.
PHILIPPIANS 3:20 NLV

Understand:

- Do you ever worry about or are you afraid of dying?
- In today's scripture reading, how did Paul view death?

Apply:

Today's reading is part of Paul's letter to the Christian church in Philippi. Paul suffered in prison for preaching about Jesus, but instead of worrying about dying, Paul looked forward to the day when Jesus would come for him and he would be made perfect. He encouraged all Christians to think this way.

We are made citizens of heaven by accepting Jesus as our Savior. Jesus said in John 14:1–3 (NLV), "Do not let your heart be troubled. You have put your trust in God, put your trust in Me also. There are many rooms in My Father's house. . . . I am going away to make a place for you. After I go and make a place for you, I will come back and take you with Me. Then you may be where I am."

The idea of dying and being taken somewhere unfamiliar can lead to worry and fear; but if we think, as Paul did, of it being the perfect end to our imperfect lives, heaven is something to look forward to.

Add to your identity that you are a citizen of heaven. While on earth, you are like the Israelites traveling to the Promised Land, and when you get there—oh my, how wonderful it will be!

Pray:

Lord Jesus, thank You for my citizenship in heaven and for preparing a place for me there. I will live my life fully while anticipating the amazing things You have waiting for me when I come home to You.

THE BOOK OF LIFE

Read Psalm 139

Key Verse:

Your eyes saw me before I was put together. And all the days of my life were written in Your book before any of them came to be.

PSALM 139:16 NLV

Understand:

- What did you learn from Psalm 139 about your relationship with God?
- Is your name written in the Book of Life? How do you know?

Psalm 139 is a powerful psalm about our relationship with God. It tells of how well He knows His children—their hearts, their thoughts, their actions, and the words they will say even before they speak. God understands us in ways we can't. He planned our lives well before we were born.

Today's key verse mentions God's book—the Book of Life—in which God has planned all the days of our lives. Moses spoke of it in Exodus 32:31–33. Psalm 56:8 says God records each of our tears in His book. In Daniel 12:1–4, God told Daniel about the book in the end times: "Your people will be saved from the trouble, every last one found written in the Book" (verse 1 MSG). You can read more about the book in the end times in Revelation 20:11–15.

Your name is written in God's Book of Life, and it remains there forever when you accept Christ's gift of salvation. God loves you so much! He wants your relationship with Him to strengthen each day. Try making every day a good one as He chronicles your life in His book.

Pray:

O God, You know everything about me. You planned my life well before I was conceived. You knew my name and wrote it in Your book. Even now, You record my every action, word, and thought because You watch over me and love me. May I live each day in ways that please You.

I HAVE CONFIDENCE

Read 2 Chronicles 32:1-8

Key Verses:

"Be strong and courageous. Do not be afraid or discouraged because of the king of Assyria and the vast army with him, for there is a greater power with us than with him. With him is only the arm of flesh, but with us is the LORD our God to help us and to fight our battles." And the people gained confidence from what Hezekiah the king of Judah said.

2 CHRONICLES 32:7–8 NIV

Understand:

- How do you prepare when you know trouble is coming?
- Do you have confidence that everything will be okay?

Apply:

King Hezekiah was faithful to God. He did his best to do what was right and good. In 2 Chronicles 32:1–8, when the king of Assyria and his army were coming to wage war against Jerusalem, Hezekiah fortified the city walls, built lookout towers, and made sure his men had enough shields and weapons. He cut off the water supply outside the city so the enemy wouldn't have water.

The people of Jerusalem worried they weren't strong enough to overcome the Assyrians. So Hezekiah called them together and spoke the words in today's key verses. His words gave the people confidence.

Your heavenly Father wants you to be confident, courageous, and strong. When worry strips away your confidence, remember, as Hezekiah did, that God's power is greater than anything that tries to destroy you. God will help you fight your battles. Your confidence comes from Him. Listen. He speaks to your heart as a father speaks to his child: "I will be right here helping you. You can do this! Everything will be okay."

Pray:

Dear Lord, I worry sometimes about what might happen. Please make me confident that You will guide me through whatever lies ahead and that everything will be okay.

I AM STRONG

Read Esther 4

Key Verse:

"For if you keep quiet at this time, help will come to the Jews from another place. But you and your father's house will be destroyed. Who knows if you have not become queen for such a time as this?"

Esther 4:14 NLV

Understand:

- Do you worry about "getting involved" and standing up for what's right?
- What would you be willing to risk to save the lives of your people?

Apply:

If you read the entire book of Esther, you will learn that an evil man tricked King Ahasuerus into agreeing that every Jew in his kingdom should be killed. Queen Esther, the king's wife, was a Jew, but she had kept this a secret from the king. In today's reading, Esther's relative Mordecai told her of the king's plan, and he begged for her help. "Who knows?" he said. "Maybe you became queen for such a time as this." Esther worried about what the king would do when she confessed that she was a Jew, but she gathered her strength and asked for prayer. "If I die, I die!" she said.

Esther is an example of what it means to be strong. She asked for prayer and then did what she knew was right. It meant taking a risk. Still, she gathered her strength and took action.

Do you worry that you might not be strong enough to face big problems or challenges? God will give you all the strength you need. Who knows? Maybe you were born for such a time as this. Your reaction might be a key part in God's perfect plan.

Pray:

O God, build up my strength so I can face the unknown without worry or fear. Give me courage to stand up for what's right, no matter what.

I AM ABLE

Read Mark 9:14-27

Key Verses:

"If You can do anything to help us, take pity on us!" Jesus said to him, "Why do you ask Me that? The one who has faith can do all things."
MARK 9:22–23 NLV

Understand:

- Do you believe that faith in Jesus strengthens your ability to achieve tough goals?
- Have you accomplished something you thought impossible?
- Are you worried that something you are praying for is impossible?

Apply:

The dad in Mark 9:14–27 worried that it was impossible for his son to be healed. He said to Jesus, "If You can do anything to help, please do!" Imagine saying that to Jesus. Of course, we know something the boy's father didn't. He was asking the Son of God if He was able to help, but this was before Jesus' death on the cross and His resurrection. Today, we are certain that Jesus is able to do anything, and especially the impossible.

"You people of this day have no faith," Jesus said in Mark 9:19 (NLV). He says it to us too. We have little faith in our ability to attain lofty goals or to meet tough challenges because we don't have enough faith in the Lord. Paul told us in Philippians 4:13 (NLV), "I can do all things because Christ gives me the strength." In the literal sense, we can't do things that are physically impossible for humans to do; but with faith in Christ we can reach seemingly impossible goals.

As you continue to ponder the question *Who am I?*, add that you are able. Jesus can give you the ability, strength, and courage to overcome challenges and accomplish your goals.

Pray:

Lord God, some goals appear so big that I haven't even tried. Which do You want me to strive for? Strengthen my willingness to try. With You and I working together, I know I am able.

I AM ENOUGH

Read Exodus 3:1–14

Key Verse:

And God said to Moses, "I AM WHO I AM." And He said, "Say to the Israelites, 'I AM has sent me to you.'"

Exodus 3:14 NLV

Understand:

- What do you think God meant when He said, "I AM WHO I AM"?
- Do you ever worry that you are not enough just as you are?
- How can you get rid of any negative feelings you have about yourself?

Apply:

God describes Himself simply as I AM. But there is nothing simple about God's character. He is all-powerful, all-knowing, and present everywhere. God is in total control of everything in the universe as well as in heaven. He has always been, and He will be forever. His power and greatness are beyond anything we can comprehend.

The God who spoke to Moses from the burning bush is the same God who speaks to you today.

He knows you in ways you don't know yourself. He hears and answers your prayers. He created you and calls Himself your Father. He teaches, guides, and leads you, and He protects you from evil because He has power over every problem and obstacle that gets in your way. God gives you courage, confidence, and strength in hard times—and He loves you. In Isaiah 46:4 (NLV), He said, "Even when you are old I will be the same. And even when your hair turns white, I will help you. I will take care of what I have made. I will carry you, and will save you." If you find yourself worrying that you aren't good enough, smart enough, or loved enough, remember that you are, because you are His.

Pray:

Dear God, I am enough because I am Yours. Help me to believe that! Remind me every day that it is enough to be Your child and to be loved and led by You.

GOD IS MY COMFORT

Read Psalm 94:16–23

Key Verse:

When my worry is great within me,
Your comfort brings joy to my soul.
PSALM 94:19 NLV

Understand:

- Do you worry about evil in the world today?
- When you feel worried, what brings you comfort?

Apply:

Every day we hear of evil acts done by those who have no regard for others. The innocent are victims, and it makes us angry! We ask ourselves, *What would we do without faith in our God?* There is comfort knowing that He is our protector. God promises that in His own time He will punish the wrongdoers. And in the meantime, His loving-kindness will hold us up and hold us together when everything else is falling apart. Psalm 94:16–23 is a good passage to remember when we worry that evil surrounds us. It reminds us that God stands up for His children. He is our safe place.

Before He went back to heaven, Jesus told His disciples that God would send them "another Comforter" who would be with them forever (John 14:16 KJV). The Comforter is the Holy Spirit, and He is our helper. The Holy Spirit is the Spirit of God working in and through us. He helps us with our worries, guides our thoughts, and even prays for us. The Spirit is that voice in our hearts that calms us, reassures us, and reminds us that God is ours forever and trouble lasts only for a while.

When we believe that God is all that He says He is, then we know we are protected by His power, and our worries can turn to joy.

Pray:

Father, there is such evil in the world today, people hurting each other through actions and words. It worries me and makes me angry. But, God, I find comfort knowing that You will protect me and bring justice to the ones who do wrong.

LOVE CASTS OUT FEAR

Read 1 John 4:7–18

Key Verse:

There is no room in love for fear. Well-formed love banishes fear. Since fear is crippling, a fearful life—fear of death, fear of judgment—is one not yet fully formed in love.

1 John 4:18 MSG

Understand:

- How is God's love different from human love?
- How is God's love made complete in us?
- How can applying what you learned in today's reading help you overcome your worries and fears?

Apply:

First John 4:7–18 is an important lesson about God's love. John said that when we accept Jesus as Savior, God comes to live inside our hearts. Then His love is made perfect in us, a love so perfect that it can't be compared to human love. Simply put, John told us, God is love (verse 8).

With God living within us, our goal is to rely

on His love the way Jesus did while here on earth: surrendering every worry and fear to God and trusting Him with the outcome. If we can learn to trust in God's love the way Jesus did, then we will find peace when we feel worried or afraid.

Fear is Satan telling us that something awful might happen. God's perfect love casts out fear, but only if we stop dwelling on Satan's words and surrender our worries to God. When we do that, it is like completing a circle: Our imperfect human love and God's love connect, and His love is made complete in us. Work hard to complete that circle. When worry and fear occupy your thoughts, rely on God's love to protect you, give you hope, and bring you peace.

Pray:

Dear God, open my heart to receive Your perfect love. Teach me to rely on Your love to cast out all my worries and fears, and Lord, give me peace.

A MOTHER'S PAIN

Read John 19:17–27

Key Verse:

Near the cross of Jesus stood his mother, his mother's sister, Mary the wife of Clopas, and Mary Magdalene.
JOHN 19:25 NIV

Understand:

- How did Jesus provide support for Mary from the cross?
- If you're a mother, who can you turn to for support when you worry about your children?

Apply:

There is no greater love on earth than a mother's love for her children. There is no greater worry either. Mothers want their children to be safe, happy, and well. When their children suffer, moms suffer too.

Imagine Mary's worry and pain as she saw her son Jesus being tortured, sentenced to death, and dying on the cross. She stood at the foot of the cross unable to do anything but surrender her boy to His heavenly Father. She had prayed for Jesus throughout His life, knowing that God had a unique plan for Him. Did she know that God's plan meant Jesus would suffer and die in the worst possible way? Jesus saw Mary standing there with her sister and Mary Magdalene. John was there too. God had provided loved ones to care for Mary on the worst day of her life, and from the cross, Jesus assured Mary that she was not alone.

Maybe you are a mom praying for your child to be delivered from evil, suffering, or pain. Moms all over the world share your worries. Reach out to family members and friends for support. Ask them to join you in prayer. It's hard not knowing God's plan for your children, but you can find comfort knowing that God is holding them and loving them, and He is holding and loving you too.

Pray:

O Lord, I am so worried about my child. Lead me to people who will support me and pray with me. I surrender my child to You, Lord, trusting that Your plan is good.

A MOTHER'S JOY

Read Matthew 28:1–10

Key Verse:

They went away from the grave in a hurry.
They were afraid and yet had much joy.
They ran to tell the news to His followers.
MATTHEW 28:8 NLV

Understand:

- If you're a mother, how can Christ's resurrection give you hope when you worry about your children?
- Can you think of a time when God unexpectedly turned your sadness to joy?

Apply:

The story of Jesus' death and resurrection is one you may know well. But let's look at it from another perspective, one that requires some imagination:

Mary Magdalene and "the other Mary" went to Jesus' tomb and were met there by an angel. "The angel said to the women, 'Do not be afraid. I know you are looking for Jesus Who was nailed to the cross. He is not here! He has risen from the dead. . . . Run fast and tell His followers that He is risen' " (Matthew 28:5–7 NLV). Although the Gospels don't say that Jesus' mother was "the other Mary" or that she saw Him after He rose from the dead, surely she was one of the first to hear the news from her friends. Imagine Mary's joy knowing that her boy had escaped death and that because He had, she would be with Him forever in heaven.

Today's passage gives hope to all mothers. If you have worries and are praying for your children, keep praying, keep hoping. Have faith that they will be resurrected from their troubles. Keep asking the Lord to turn your worries to joy.

Pray:

Lord Jesus, just as You rose from the grave, I know it is possible for my child to rise from trouble. I will keep hoping and praying. Lord, lead me to the day when my worries turn to joy.

ELDERLY PARENTS

Read 1 Timothy 5:1-8

Key Verse:

If a woman whose husband has died has children or grandchildren, they are the ones to care for her. In that way, they can pay back to their parents the kindness that has been shown to them. God is pleased when this is done.

1 Timothy 5:4 NLV

Understand:

- What is the key message of 1 Timothy 5:1–8?
- Do you worry about caring for your parents in their old age?

In today's passage, Paul spoke about having respect for each other and how to treat the elderly. Paul specifically addressed caring for widows, but his message can also apply to adult children caring for their parents. God is pleased when He sees children repaying their parents with kindness. First Timothy 5:8 (TLB) says, "But anyone who won't care for his own relatives when they need help, especially those living in his own family, has no right to say he is a Christian."

One worry many of us share is losing our parents. Whatever our age, the idea of being without Mom and Dad is one we avoid. We worry also about caring for them and taking on more responsibility for their well-being. If they should become unable to care for themselves, we worry whether we can provide what they need. The idea of caregiving is daunting, but if faced with it, we can rely on God's faithfulness to get us through. God has His way of providing for a caregiver's needs whether it be additional help, resources, or rest. If you are currently caring for your parents, draw strength from the Lord. If your parents are happy and healthy, celebrate that today, and don't set your worries on tomorrow.

Pray:

Father, keep me vigilant to my parents' needs, and provide me with strength and guidance to care for them as they age.

WHEN I AM OLD

Read Psalm 71:1-20

Key Verses:

And now, in my old age, don't set me aside. Don't forsake me now when my strength is failing. My enemies are whispering, "God has forsaken him! Now we can get him. There is no one to help him now!" O God, don't stay away! Come quickly! Help!

Psalm 71:9–12 TLB

Understand:

- What did you learn about aging from today's reading?
- How can you keep a positive attitude about growing old?

Apply:

If you are sixty or older, you probably worry about growing old. In today's reading, David was an old man worried about enemies overpowering him in his weakness. In our key verses, we sense distress in David's voice. (This could very well be us in our old age: "Oh, God, I'm becoming weak. The enemies are chasing me—things I'm not able to do anymore, aches and pains, illnesses, even death!

Come quickly! Help!") But through the worries, David remembered the many times God rescued him and gave him strength. David was alive, and he still had a purpose.

The saying "Age is a state of mind" is true. If we keep our minds set on God's faithfulness and remember that He isn't done with us yet, we don't need to worry about aging. Following is a Bible verse to keep in your heart for when you grow old: "I will be your God through all your lifetime, yes, even when your hair is white with age. I made you and I will care for you. I will carry you along and be your Savior" (Isaiah 46:4 TLB).

Pray:

Dear God, when I grow old I will draw my strength from You. Until You call me home, I will do my best to serve You and lead others to know You.

AN OLDER WOMAN'S PURPOSE

Read Titus 2:1–8

Key Verses:

Older women are to teach the young women to love their husbands and children. They are to teach them to think before they act, to be pure.

Titus 2:4–5 NLV

Understand:

- Why is it important for older people to share with younger generations what they have learned about right living?
- Can you think of several younger women in your life who could grow as Christians from your teaching?

If you are an older woman worried that you don't have a purpose anymore, think again! In Paul's letter to Titus, he said older women are to teach younger women to lead productive Christian lives.

Older women have acquired much wisdom while living life and raising their families. The wisdom they impart to younger family members and friends is of great value. One way to mentor younger women is by example, showing what it means to be Christian by our actions and words. Another is to form friendships and engage more often with younger women. Coffee dates are great for having conversations about life. Stories about how God led us and intervened in our lives can be a gateway to talking about God's faithfulness and love.

As Christians, our most important purpose is to lead others to Christ and help them live according to His teachings. Embrace your purpose today. The words you speak and the example you set for younger women could make an impact on their lives forever.

Pray:

Father, thank You for reminding me that my greatest purpose is to lead others to You. Please help me share with younger women the wisdom I have gained from many years of knowing You. Open their hearts, Lord, as I share what it's like to go through life with You.

THE SACRIFICES WE MAKE

Read Ruth 1:1–18

Key Verses:

But Ruth said, "Do not beg me to leave you or turn away from following you. I will go where you go. I will live where you live. Your people will be my people. And your God will be my God. I will die where you die, and there I will be buried. So may the Lord do the same to me, and worse, if anything but death takes me from you."

Ruth 1:16–17 NLV

Understand:

- If you were Ruth, a young woman with your whole life ahead of you, would you have returned home, or would you have stayed with your mother-in-law?
- How do you feel about sacrifices you have made for your family members?

Women know what it means to make sacrifices for their families. Each day, they give up their own wants and needs for their loved ones. Children require attention. Husbands do too. Sometimes siblings, parents, and other family members need support.

Women often make sacrifices because they are motivated by love.

The Bible story of Naomi and Ruth is a beautiful example. Ruth willingly gave up returning home, and maybe finding someone to marry, and chose instead to care for her elderly mother-in-law. The loving words she spoke to Naomi in Ruth 1:16–17 must have brought the old woman comfort and eased her worries. If you read the entire book of Ruth, you will see how God rewarded Ruth for her selflessness.

Sacrificing our needs for the needs of others isn't always easy, but it is one way to show obedience to God and serve Him by serving others.

Pray:

Dear Jesus, You gave Your life for me out of love. Help me to reflect Your example of love and to find joy in selflessness, even if it means sacrificing something I want.

GOD MADE ME BEAUTIFUL

Read Ezekiel 16:10–15

Key Verse:

"Your name became known among the nations because of your beauty. For it was perfect because of My shining-greatness which I had given to you," says the Lord God.

Ezekiel 16:14 NLV

Understand:

- Using a scale of 1–10, how important is it for you to look beautiful?
- What is your idea of true beauty?
- Do you believe that God thinks you are beautiful just as you are?

Apply:

In Ezekiel 16, God compared the city of Jerusalem to a beautiful woman. God had created Jerusalem just the way He wanted her. In His eyes, she was perfect. If you read beyond today's passage, you will discover that Jerusalem became obsessed with her beauty and used it in ways that displeased God.

Many women today worry about their looks. Some have surgeries to change their bodies, and still, when they look in the mirror, they aren't satisfied.

Peter wrote in 1 Peter 3:4 (NLV), "Your beauty should come from the inside. It should come from the heart. This is the kind that lasts. Your beauty should be a gentle and quiet spirit. In God's sight this is of great worth and no amount of money can buy it." The average woman spends hundreds, even thousands, each year on skin care, hair care, clothing, jewelry, and makeup. But no amount she spends to be beautiful compares with the beauty she was born with.

God created each of us beautiful in His sight. True beauty is found inside our hearts, and it radiates outward in loving-kindness when we speak and act to please God. When we concentrate more on cultivating a heart that pleases Him, then we worry less about having a beautiful body.

Pray:

Heavenly Father, please keep me from worrying more about my outer looks than my inner beauty. Give me a gentle, quiet spirit, the kind of beauty no money can buy.

FALSE TEACHING

Read Jude 17–25

Key Verse:

There is One Who can keep you from falling and can bring you before Himself free from all sin.
JUDE 24 NLV

Understand:

- Do you feel confused about what God says is right and wrong?
- How do you feel about people who disagree with your beliefs?
- How can you find peace in this deeply divided world?

Apply:

The book of Jude says that in the last days false teachers will lead people away from God's truth. They will make trouble by dividing people into groups against each other. Does that sound like what's happening in the world today? People are deeply divided over what's right and wrong, even hating each other for opposing beliefs. Some Christians have fallen for ideas coming from man rather than from God. Others are afraid of falling; false teaching has led them to confusion and worry, making them question what they've been taught about God and Christianity. But those who stay immersed in God's Word and reject what's contrary to His teaching are freed from worry. Because they're led by the Holy Spirit, nothing on earth can separate them from the truth.

Many of us are concerned about how divided we've become. We ask, "How did things get like this?" The answer is that we live in a fallen world. Our focus has shifted from God's Word to the words of man. First Corinthians 14:33 (KJV) tells us, "For God is not the author of confusion, but of peace." The only way we let go of worry and find peace is by seeking and believing God's truth. Ask God to separate you from false teaching and fill you up with His Word.

Pray:

Dear God, we live in such a confusing time. What's wrong seems right and what's right seems wrong. Guide me away from false teaching and lead me instead to the truth in Your Word.

JESUS GIVES US PEACE

Read John 16:16–33

Key Verse:

"I have told you these things so you may have peace in Me. In the world you will have much trouble. But take hope! I have power over the world!"

John 16:33 NLV

Understand:

- Are Jesus and God one with each other?
- How can you find peace when you are worried and troubled?

Apply:

Jesus often taught His followers using stories, stories that made them think about and apply His teachings to their lives. But in John 16, Jesus spoke directly to His disciples, asking if they believed He had come from God. He expressed that He and God were one. The disciples were confident that Jesus was God's Son and that everything He had told them was true. Jesus reassured them, saying, "I have told you these things so you may have peace in Me. In the world you will have much trouble. But take hope! I have power over the world!"

Jesus' words were meant not only for His disciples but for all generations. Troubles will exist until Jesus returns, but in the midst of these troubles, we can find peace by trusting that Jesus is with us and has power over the world.

Whatever worries you may have today, bring those concerns to Jesus. He never promised that we would be free from trouble, but He did promise us peace during difficult times—a peace that comes from surrendering our worries to Him and trusting in His ability to overcome them. Jesus and God are one, and with both working on your behalf, you have nothing to worry about.

Pray:

Lord Jesus, sometimes I forget that You promised me peace when I'm troubled. I dwell on my worries instead of giving them to You. Lord, You have power over my troubles. Help me to find peace by putting my trust in You.

STRESSED OUT

Read Psalm 6

Key Verse:

I am tired of crying inside myself.
All night long my pillow is wet with
tears. I flood my bed with them.
PSALM 6:6 NLV

Understand:

- How can you apply David's prayer in Psalm 6 to your own life?
- Where do your thoughts go when you feel stressed out?

David's prayer in Psalm 6 shows us a man stressed out and overwhelmed by his troubles. David's thoughts go round and round as he dwells on his misery. At first, he assumed God was angry with him. "Be kind to me, O Lord," he said (verse 2 NLV). Then David described for God how miserable he felt—as if God didn't already know. Finally, he begged, "Set my soul free. Save me" (verse 4 NLV).

David had fallen into that dark place where he thought everybody hated him. But then, remembering that God heard his prayer and his plea for help,

David pulled himself up. He knew that God loved him. God would save him from those who hurt him, and God would put them to shame.

We've all been there, haven't we, in that place where stress overwhelms us and makes us wonder if we'll live through it? Worrisome thoughts grow big within us until, finally, we say, "I'm tired of crying and feeling this way." That's when our thoughts turn to God.

Satan loves shoving us into a state of despair, but he hates when we remember that God has power over him. We find strength when shifting our thoughts from expressions of anguish to *God will get that evil one! God will take care of him and all the trouble he brings.* We could save ourselves a lot of worry if as soon as troublesome thoughts begin, we turn them over to God.

Pray:

Dear God, free my soul from the bondage of stress. Forgive me for overreacting and dwelling on my misery.

FINDING BALANCE

Read Ecclesiastes 3:1–13

Key Verse:

There is a time for everything, and a season for every activity under the heavens.

Ecclesiastes 3:1 NIV

Understand:

- What takes up most of your time?
- What do you notice about your attitude when your life is out of balance?

Apply:

Just as we can't change the order that God ordained for spring giving way to summer, summer to fall, and fall to winter, we also can't alter the seasons that God has planned for our lives. Life's rhythm and flow are circular. Ecclesiastes 3:1–8 illustrates this by showing how good times give way to bad times, and bad times yield to good.

The key to finding peace in all seasons is learning to accept things as they come and countering what we perceive as "bad" with God's goodness. In Ecclesiastes 3:9–13, Solomon suggested that we cannot predict what life will bring, so we should make the most of it by remembering that life is a gift from God. This involves finding balance and not allowing anxiety, worry, and stress to overwhelm us, robbing us of laughter and joy.

It's important to carve out time in our busy days for prayer and meditation, for fellowship with family and friends, and for rest, relaxation, and fun.

We can bring more balance to our lives by inviting God into our daily routines. We do this by trusting in His plans and timing, focusing on our blessings, and appreciating the good in life. Balance is also about finding joy in simple things, spending quiet time with God, and setting priorities that honor Him.

How are you doing at balancing your life? Are there things you need to change?

Pray:

Lord God, guide me to use my time in ways that honor You. Teach me to discern my priorities and make time for work, rest, and play.

THE GLASS CEILING

Read Ephesians 6:5-9

Key Verse:

Be happy as you work. Do your work as for the Lord, not for men.

EPHESIANS 6:7 NLV

Understand:

- What, if any, are your career goals?
- What might be stopping you from getting ahead at work?
- What part does God play in the work you do each day?

Apply:

The glass ceiling—it's that invisible barrier that some women believe keeps them from advancing in their careers. They work to please their bosses, putting pressure on themselves, hoping that it will help them get ahead. Sometimes it works. Sometimes it doesn't. And when it doesn't, there's the glass ceiling to blame.

The truth is that there is no glass ceiling when we strive to please God, because with Him all things are possible. Paul discussed this in Ephesians 6, where he advised us to work as diligently for our bosses as we would for the Lord. Instead of concentrating on breaking through a glass ceiling, we should focus on allowing God to guide us to where He wants us to go. We should find happiness in our work, knowing that whatever good thing we do, God will pay us for it.

Life isn't always fair, especially in the workplace. Paul spoke also to leaders, reminding them to treat their workers well and to remember that God doesn't treat leaders differently than He does their employees.

If your work has you worried about whether you can get ahead, maybe God has other plans for you. Keep praying and asking Him to lead you. In the meantime, do your best work, so at the end of the day God can look at you and say, "Well done!"

Pray:

Heavenly Father, I want a career that satisfies me, and I know I will find it on the path You have set for me. Lead me there. As I go about my work, may I always focus on pleasing You.

MORE OR LESS?

Read Matthew 25:14–30

Key Verse:

"For the man who has will have more given to him. He will have more than enough. The man who has nothing, even what he has will be taken away."

MATTHEW 25:29 NLV

Understand:

- What did you learn from today's reading?
- Can Jesus' story be applied to more than money?
- Are you a saver, or are you a risk taker?

Apply:

Many who read Jesus' parable about the servants and the money conclude it is about making wise investments to increase their wealth—in other words, they think it is about managing their money as if they were managing it for the Lord. Being wise about our investments is always good advice, but today's passage has a deeper meaning. It is about investing ourselves in God's kingdom.

Believers are all on a journey to heaven. God gives each of us unique gifts to help His kingdom grow here on earth. Whether it is money, skills, talents, or something else, we are to use our gifts in big ways instead of allowing them to become stagnant. Then, when we get to heaven someday, we will see how using our gifts enriched the lives of others and helped further God's kingdom.

Investing requires responsibility and taking risks. Often we are afraid of risk taking, worried that it might lead to failure or loss. We needn't worry if the risk means strengthening our gifts—our skills, talents, abilities—or if the risk might lead others to Christ. Ask God to help you grow your gifts so you'll have even more to give.

Pray:

Dear God, if a risk is one You want me to take, help me to step out in faith. Teach me to grow my gifts so I'll have even more to give.

USING YOUR GIFTS

Read Romans 12:3-8

Key Verse:

We all have different gifts that God has given to us by His loving-favor. We are to use them.

ROMANS 12:6 NLV

Understand:

- What are you good at? What special abilities has God given you?
- How confident are you to share your skills and talents with others?

Apply:

The key message in today's reading is that we should use the special skills, talents, and abilities that God gave us, and we should use them willingly.

It's easy to share what we're good at if we have confidence. But sometimes we worry that our special gifts aren't good enough to share. Think of a child's first recital. Some children have no worries about performing in front of a group. Other children are worried and afraid. They cry and beg, "Mommy, please don't make me do this!" Fear is our enemy. It stops us from serving God and sharing our gifts with others.

When God creates each person, He puts within them a multitude of things they are good at. While all of us have these special gifts, how we use them is unique. God gives us the ability, and we get to choose how to use it.

Make a list of your gifts. Are you good at parenting, teaching, fixing things, coaching, music, art, writing. . . ? What are some creative ways you can share your gifts? Think outside the box. What characteristics of your personality could you use to help or enrich the lives of others? Don't allow fear to get in your way. Be confident. Even if your gifts aren't well refined, they will improve the more you use them.

Pray:

Dear God, give me power over worry, shyness, and fear so I can use my gifts to the fullest. Bless me with creative ideas for sharing my gifts with others.

FINANCIAL WORRIES

Read Job 42:10–16

Key Verse:

The Lord returned to Job all the things that he had lost. . . . The Lord gave Job twice as much as he had before.
JOB 42:10 NLV

Understand:

- Job had been rich, but he lost everything. How would you react if that happened to you?
- Why do you think God restored all that Job lost?

Apply:

Why do bad things happen to good people? Often, we can't know. In the book of Job, it was because God allowed Job's faith to be tested.

Job had been a very rich man, but he lost everything. His friends offered their ideas about why Job was suffering. It *had* to be because of something he had done. Job's wife even suggested that Job just curse God and die. But, although Job asked God why, he never stopped having faith. God rewarded Job's faithfulness and gave him twice as much as he'd had before.

Maybe you are suffering with financial worries through no fault of your own. You did whatever you could to hold on to what you had and watched it slip away. What now? Hold on to God's Word and His promises. Keep praying and trusting that God is fighting this battle for you. Stand firm in faith, as Job did, and believe that in His own way God will restore what you've lost. Satan will do all he can to get you to question God's goodness and God's ability to save you. Don't listen. Ask God to deliver you from evil and to help you stay strong. Trust Him to provide for you and to lead you to people who can help.

Pray:

Lord, I don't know why You are allowing me to go through this financial crisis, but I have faith You will bring me through it. Please calm my worries and lead me. Connect me with people who can help. Keep me strong so I won't fall into Satan's traps.

FAITH FAILURE

Read Luke 22:28-34

Key Verses:

Peter said to Jesus, "Lord, I am ready to go to prison and to die with You!" Jesus said, "I tell you, Peter, a rooster will not crow today before you will say three times that you do not know Me."

Luke 22:33–34 NLV

Understand:

- What did you learn about human weakness from today's passage?
- Can you think of a time when you thought your faith was strong and discovered that it wasn't?
- How can you reestablish your faith when it fails you?

Apply:

The setting was the Last Supper. Jesus was preparing His twelve disciples for His death, and He warned the men that Satan would test their faith. He specifically addressed Peter, the most headstrong of His followers. "I have prayed that you will not lose your faith!" Jesus told him. "Help your brothers be stronger when you come back to Me." Imagine

Peter saying, "Lose my faith! Come back to You? Are you kidding—I would have to die first." But fear did make Peter lose his faith, and just hours later, he denied knowing Jesus. This wasn't the first time fear got in his way. Read the story of Peter walking on water in Matthew 14:22–32. (Paul struggled with faith too. Read about it in Romans 7:14–25.)

We are like Peter, wanting to stay faith-strong but failing. Following Jesus isn't easy. If you worry about your faith being strong enough, don't. Sometimes your faith will fail you. Jesus understands. He will forgive you, just as He did Peter.

Pray:

Lord Jesus, like Peter I've believed that nothing can diminish my faith in You, but then I fell. When my faith fails, I feel guilty. I know You forgive me, Lord. Please help me to forgive myself. I want to be strong, but sometimes being human gets in the way.

NOT GUILTY

Read John 8:2-11

Key Verses:

Jesus stood up and said to her, "Woman, where are those who spoke against you? Has no man said you are guilty?" She said, "No one, Sir." Jesus said to her, "Neither do I say you are guilty. Go on your way and do not sin again."

JOHN 8:10–11 NLV

Understand:

- Are you guilty of "casting stones" at others for their sins?
- Are you holding on to guilt for wrong things you have done?

Apply:

The Pharisees brought to court a woman accused of adultery. The law said she should be stoned to death. They asked Jesus what He thought. "[Jesus] stood up and said, 'Anyone of you who is without sin can throw the first stone" (John 8:7 NLV). One by one, the men walked away. Jesus stood with the woman in the empty room. "Has no man said you are guilty?" He asked. The woman answered, "No one, Sir." Then Jesus said, "Neither do I say you are guilty. Go on your way and do not sin again."

The obvious lesson is not to cast stones so easily, because none of us are without sin. But there's another, less obvious lesson. The woman never said that she didn't commit the sin. Still, Jesus didn't condemn her. He found her not guilty. This foreshadowed the gift of redemption that was coming, salvation from our sins through Him.

Our sins can cause us perpetual guilt and shame. Some of us worry that sin will keep us from entering heaven. Jesus says, "Not guilty!" As soon as we accept Him as Savior, our guilt is washed away, not just once, but forever.

Pray:

Lord Jesus, I'm guilty of sin but also guilty of holding on to guilt and shame for the wrong things I've done. Thank You, Lord, for Your gift of unconditional forgiveness. My sins are washed away. My slate is wiped clean!

GOD BELIEVES IN ME

Read Acts 9:1–19

Key Verse:

The Lord said to him, "Go! This man is the one I have chosen to carry My name among the people who are not Jews and to their kings and to Jews."

Acts 9:15 NLV

Understand:

- Is it possible for those who have worked against God to be saved?
- Do you think God believes in your ability to do His work here on earth?

Apply:

Have you wondered if God believes that you can accomplish great things? You might think you are least likely to be someone God believes in—but you're wrong. God believes in all of us. He knows He can turn our lives around, so we in turn can serve Him and do His work on earth.

Paul was least likely. Before they called him Paul, he was Saul, a Jesus hater who wanted to destroy all the Christians. In Acts 9:1–19, Paul was on the road to Damascus, where he planned to arrest the Christians there and take them back to Jerusalem in chains. But God intervened. This man—this evil man—was the one God chose to become the greatest missionary of all time. If God could believe in Paul, then He can believe in us too.

Maybe you worry that God doesn't think you are good enough to serve Him. Turn that worry around! If you are a Christian, God has already chosen you for a purpose. He is ready to give you a mission if you are willing. With confidence in yourself—and more importantly, in Him—stand tall and say, "Yes, God, I am willing." Then ask Him to show you the way.

Pray:

God, I've wondered how I could ever be good enough to serve You here on earth. Yet You believe I am. You already have a mission ready for me. I'm willing, Lord! Use me. I am able, so show me the way.

IMPRISONED

Read Acts 12:5–17

Key Verse:

As Peter began to see what was happening, he said to himself, "Now I am sure the Lord has sent His angel and has taken me out of the hands of Herod. He has taken me also from all the things the Jews wanted to do to me."

Acts 12:11 NLV

Understand:

- What emotions do you think Peter experienced while in prison?
- Have you ever felt trapped by worry and anxiety?

Apply:

The anxiety Peter felt in prison must have been overwhelming at times, but he found solace trusting in the Lord and knowing that others were praying for him. Imagine how wonderful Peter felt when he was freed from prison and his worries.

Those experiencing anxiety know that it feels like being in prison. Anxiety is living with constant worries and dreading what might happen next. For Peter, it was not knowing if he would be tortured and killed. Today, our anxiety comes from any number of things. Multiple worries gang up on us all at once.

The minister Alexander McLaren once said, "What does your anxiety do? It does not empty tomorrow of its sorrow, but it does empty today of its strength. It does not make you escape the evil; it makes you unfit to cope with it when it comes." If you are a prisoner of anxiety, ask others to pray for you. Ask God to free you from prison, as He did Peter. God wants you to be freed. It is another of His gifts to you. So accept His gift today. Let Him help you break free from your chains.

Pray:

Father God, I'm trapped in the prison of anxiety, and I don't know how to get out. My hope is in You. Free me from this pattern of worry. Lead me to people who will pray for me and help.

JUST BREATHE

Read Ezekiel 37:1–10

Key Verse:

Then He said to me, "Speak to the breath in My name, son of man. Tell the breath, 'The Lord God says, "Come from the four winds, O breath, and breathe on these dead bodies to make them come to life."'"

EZEKIEL 37:9 NLV

Understand:

- In this analogy of the valley of bones, what do you think the dry bones symbolize? What do you think the wind represents?
- What does Ezekiel 37:1–10 teach us about spiritual death?

Apply:

Today's reading highlights the vision God gave to the prophet Ezekiel. He showed Ezekiel a valley filled with dried-up human bones. God said to Ezekiel, "These bones are all the people of Israel. They say, 'Our bones are dried up, and our hope is gone. We are all destroyed'" (Ezekiel 37:11 NLV). When God asked Ezekiel, "Can these bones live?" Ezekiel answered, "O Lord God, only You know that" (verse 3 NLV). While Ezekiel watched, God formed skeletons from the bones and covered them with flesh and skin, but they were still dead. They had no breath until God told Ezekiel to speak to the wind in His name and tell it to breathe life into the bodies. Then they all came alive.

We can think of this story when we feel overwhelmed. Anxiety and worry lead to a spiritual death—they separate us from God's goodness. Counselors teach breathing techniques to calm anxiety. Those help, but there is something even better. We can ask the Holy Spirit to breathe new life into us.

Pray:

Lord God, I feel worried and stressed out today. I'm doing my best to relax by taking deep breaths, praying, and asking You to calm me with Your Holy Spirit. Come, Lord Jesus; fill me up with Your peace.

COMPANY'S COMING

Read Luke 10:38–42

Key Verse:

Martha was working hard getting the supper ready. She came to Jesus and said, "Do You see that my sister is not helping me? Tell her to help me."
Luke 10:40 NLV

Understand:

- Does planning for guests cause you worry and stress?
- Whom do you think you are most like, Mary or Martha?
- Is there a deadline you are working toward right now that has you feeling worried?

Apply:

We've all been there. Company is coming. Whether we're expecting dinner guests or friends are staying with us for a few days, anxiety comes with the preparations. There's so much to do. That alone makes us crabby, and our crabbiness gets worse if we don't see our family members pitching in to help. Before losing our tempers, we might say a silent prayer: *Lord, tell them to help me!* That's what Martha did, only she said the prayer aloud.

When we are worried and stressed about completing a task or working toward a deadline, Jesus might be whispering in our hearts, "You are worried and troubled about many things. Only a few things are important, even just one" (Luke 10:41–42 NLV). That one thing is Jesus. But the chaos of staying on schedule can keep us from hearing His voice.

When we are in a rush and worried about getting things done on time, even just five minutes of quiet time spent with Jesus can help. If we keep our minds on Him and remember that everything will be okay, then we can accomplish our tasks with peace.

Pray:

Jesus, I'm sorry for not seeking You when I'm busy and feeling stressed. Help me to remember to turn to You for refreshment. Nothing is more important than listening to You and keeping my mind set on You.

I'VE HAD ENOUGH!

Read 1 Kings 19:1-8

Key Verse:

The angel of God came back, shook him awake again, and said, "Get up and eat some more—you've got a long journey ahead of you."
1 Kings 19:7 MSG

Understand:

- Do you ever feel like you've had enough of trouble and worries?
- What do you do to help yourself out of sadness or depression?

Apply:

The Israelites were worshipping the false god Baal, and false prophets of Baal had been misleading the people. After a contest in which Elijah proved God as the only true God, he had all 450 prophets of Baal killed. (Read about it in 1 Kings 18.) As we begin today's reading, King Ahab's wicked wife, Jezebel, planned to murder Elijah.

Elijah ran for his life. He'd had enough of this! Enough of the idol worship, people not listening to him, and the persecution. Elijah lay down and hoped to die. "Get up!" said an angel from the Lord. So

Elijah got up, ate a little food, and lay down again. The angel appeared once more, telling Elijah to get up and eat again. Why? "You've got a long journey ahead of you."

Like Elijah, we can reach a point where we've had enough. When worry leads us to depression and getting out of bed in the morning feels impossible, a voice in our hearts urges us, "Get up! You have your whole life ahead of you."

Elijah got up, and God gave him strength to go on. God will offer the same support to you. He has good plans for you (Jeremiah 29:11). So get up! There is much more living to do.

Pray:

Father, life is so overwhelming that I don't want to get out of bed and face another day. But I will get up! I'm calling on You today to strengthen me and bring happiness to my heavy heart.

WHAT IF?

Read Nehemiah 2:1–8

Key Verse:

"Why should my face not be sad when the city, the place of my fathers' graves, lies waste and its gates destroyed by fire?"

NEHEMIAH 2:3 NLV

Understand:

- Why was Nehemiah heartsick?
- What did Nehemiah do when he heard about the destruction in Jerusalem?
- Do you ever worry about your home or city being destroyed?

Apply:

Nehemiah, a cupbearer to the king, was a Jew living in Persia when he heard from his brother in Jerusalem that the city had been destroyed by the Babylonians. After praying for its people, Nehemiah planned to return to his homeland to help with the rebuilding; but first, he had to ask the king's permission. Today's scripture reading begins there.

Nehemiah felt heartbroken when he learned that the city he loved lay in ruins. We can relate to Nehemiah's feelings when we hear about places in our country and around the world being destroyed. Wars, storms, fires, and floods all bring destruction. We feel sad for the people, and we worry about the possibility of it happening to us. The king granted Nehemiah permission to return to Jerusalem. Despite his anguish over the devastation, Nehemiah took action and worked hard to help restore the city.

Fast-forward to the New Testament. Jesus taught us not to worry or be afraid. He mentioned that we would have trouble in this world; but instead of giving in to worrying about what we can't control, we can find peace in knowing that whatever is destroyed, God is able to restore. He, alongside good people like Nehemiah, will step in and help us to rebuild.

Pray:

Lord, help me not to worry about events outside my control. I know that if the worst were to happen, You would be with me and You would make things right again.

OVERPOWERING EMOTIONS

Read 2 Samuel 19:1–8

Key Verse:

The king covered his face and cried out with a loud voice, "O my son Absalom, O Absalom, my son, my son!"
2 Samuel 19:4 NLV

Understand:

- What did you learn about emotions from today's reading?
- Have you ever felt overpowered by a negative emotion?

Apply:

The backstory is one of rebellion. Absalom, King David's son, turned against him. He wanted to kill his father and become king. Absalom gathered an army and went to war against David's army. It ended badly for Absalom when he was killed by Joab, one of David's generals.

David mourned Absalom's death so deeply that he forgot his kingly duties, and he forgot that Joab had saved his life as well as the lives of others. The servants tiptoed around the king, not wanting to add to his troubles. This went on for a long while until Joab said to David, "You act like you would be happy if we were all dead and Absalom were alive. Shape up! Speak kindly to your servants." While the people understood that the king was overcome by grief, they also needed their leader to lead. It was as if he had forgotten about them.

Our emotions—whether grief, worry, fear, or others—can become so overwhelming that they take control of our lives. This can create problems, especially when others depend on us. When a parent or leader becomes consumed by their emotions, it affects children, coworkers, and others around them. In David's situation, God sent Joab to remind him of his responsibilities to those who relied on him. His story serves as a reminder to manage our feelings, if not for ourselves, for the sake of others.

Pray:

Dear God, help me to manage my emotions. Remind me to be kind and caring in spite of how I feel and not to ignore the needs of those who depend on me.

THE ROOT OF TEMPTATION

Read James 1:13–18

Key Verse:

When you are tempted to do wrong, do not say, "God is tempting me." God cannot be tempted. He will never tempt anyone.

JAMES 1:13 NLV

Understand:

- How do you define temptation?
- Do you have trouble fighting temptation?

Apply:

The book of James is thought to be written by Jesus' half brother. It is a book filled with advice for living a Christian life. James taught us that Christianity is more than just a belief; it is putting belief into action.

When some Christians consider doing something sinful, something that will displease God, they think God is tempting them to sin. James told us not to fall for that trick. He said God will never tempt anyone.

Temptation comes from Satan. When a person gives in to sin, it opens the door for them to give in to even more temptation, and that weakens their faith. Sometimes God will allow Satan to tempt us as a way of leading us to strengthen our faith. The worry, the uneasiness that comes when we consider giving in to temptation comes from the Holy Spirit. It is God urging us not to give in. God only wants what's good for us, and we find what's good by knowing what's in the Bible and putting it into action through obedience.

Paul gave us a verse to use when facing temptation: "You have never been tempted to sin in any different way than other people. God is faithful. He will not allow you to be tempted more than you can take. But when you are tempted, He will make a way for you to keep from falling into sin" (1 Corinthians 10:13 NLV). Commit it to memory so you can put it into action.

Pray:

Lord God, I will do my best not to give in to temptation. Help me, Father, to strengthen my faith.

A HUMBLE SPIRIT

Read Job 22:21-29

Key Verse:

"Quit quarreling with God! Agree with him and you will have peace at last! His favor will surround you if you will only admit that you were wrong."
JOB 22:21 TLB

Understand:

- Do you have trouble admitting you are wrong and asking for forgiveness?
- Do you give credit to God for your accomplishments?

Pride can become our enemy when it causes us to sin. It's fine to be proud of the good work we do, the accomplishments of our children, and the skills and talents God gave us. But when pride becomes too big, it leads us away from God. When that happens, the Holy Spirit will begin speaking to us, trying to get us to turn from pride toward humility. Satan won't let go easily, though. If we listen to him, he will give us reasons to excuse our pride. We might begin arguing with ourselves about whether our pride is sin; we might even argue with God. Pride never wants us to admit that we are wrong.

"I was wrong"—those words are like music to God's ears. Giving up our pride for humility ends the spiritual war inside us and brings us peace. When we admit our wrongdoing and work to set things right, God is pleased.

God blesses the humble. Jesus said, "For everyone who tries to honor himself shall be humbled; and he who humbles himself shall be honored" (Luke 14:11 TLB). Humility is one of Jesus' characteristics, and we should strive to be like Him.

If you worry that you are a little too prideful, talk with God about it. Learn to give Him credit for all the good things you do.

Pray:

Heavenly Father, You are the source of anything that brings me pride. Bless me, Father, with a gentle, humble spirit.

HABAKKUK'S PRAYER

Read Habakkuk 3

Key Verses:

Though the cherry trees don't blossom and the strawberries don't ripen, though the apples are worm-eaten and the wheat fields stunted, though the sheep pens are sheepless and the cattle barns empty, I'm singing joyful praise to God. I'm turning cartwheels of joy to my Savior God.

Habakkuk 3:17–18 msg

Understand:

- Is God good even when evil is all around us?
- Do you find it difficult to praise God when things aren't going your way?

The prophet Habakkuk lived in a time similar to ours. Bad things were happening all around him. People felt worried and afraid, and God's Word was being ignored. Life in Israel was a mess, and Habakkuk asked God why He didn't do something about it. As much as Habakkuk prayed, nothing changed. He begged God to be kind and fix things, as He had done for Habakkuk's ancestors. Then, finally,

Habakkuk remembered that God is good even when nothing else is. He turned his prayers of complaint to prayers of praise.

When everything goes wrong, it's not unusual to complain to God and ask why He won't turn things around. In times like these, it's important to remember that God is still good. In His own time and way, He always makes things right.

If you have been praying about your worries, try turning your prayers toward praise. Find joy in the Lord—if for no other reason than He is your Savior and He loves you so much.

Pray:

Dear God, I've been praying, asking You to fix things, and still, nothing has changed. I've asked You why, all the while forgetting that You are always good; Your timing is always perfect. Father, I praise You for Your goodness. My heart is filled with joy because You are my Savior and You love me.

WHAT GOD WANTS

Read 1 Thessalonians 5:16–25

Key Verses:

Be full of joy all the time. Never stop praying. In everything give thanks. This is what God wants you to do because of Christ Jesus.

1 Thessalonians 5:16–18 NLV

Understand:

- What do you think God wants from you?
- Have you worried that you don't do enough to please God?

Apply:

Paul's letters are filled with information about how God wants us to live. Paul often wrote about how to please God. While all his words are instructional, important, and good, the whole amount of his advice can be daunting. God wants much from us, and trying to please Him in all we do can create stress and worry. While God expects us to "keep away from everything that even looks like sin" (1 Thessalonians 5:22 NLV), He knows we'll fail sometimes. We are all sinners, and as hard as we try, we sometimes give in to what's wrong.

In today's key verses, Paul told us never to stop praying and in everything to give thanks. This is something we *can* do! When we are weak, we can pray. When things are going wrong, we can thank God for all that is good and right. Maybe we can't be filled with joy all the time, but we can try our best to find joy in the little things God does for us each day.

We needn't worry if we don't fulfill God's will perfectly. He understands. That's why He gave us Jesus. In good times and in bad, keep praying and keep giving thanks. That is what God wants us to do.

Pray:

Heavenly Father, I worry at times that I don't do enough to please You. I've realized that I can't please You all the time, but I can keep talking with You, learning from You, and praising You.

PROVE IT!

Read Judges 6:11–17

Key Verses:

Gideon said to Him, "O Lord, how can I save Israel? See, my family is the least in Manasseh. And I am the youngest in my father's house." But the Lord said to him, "For sure I will be with you. You will destroy Midian as one man." Gideon said to Him, "If I have found favor in Your eyes, show me something to prove that it is You Who speaks with me."

JUDGES 6:15–17 NLV

Understand:

- How often do you think that you have no power over your problems?
- Have you ever asked God to prove Himself to you?

Apply:

Some problems seem too big to overcome. When trouble surrounds us, we might doubt that God is with us. We tell ourselves, *If He were, this trouble wouldn't have happened.* Trouble can overpower us to the extent that we feel small and insignificant. What if God appeared to us and said, "I have given you power over this situation. Use it! For sure, I will be with you"? How would we react? Would we be like Gideon and ask God to prove it was really Him speaking?

Doubt is our enemy. It drains our faith and allows us to worry that whatever we face we can't fight it and win. God says otherwise. He is our strength. Maybe we can't fix the situation, but we can be strong in prayer and believe that God can do it. We can assume an attitude of emotional strength and surety that our trouble will pass. And, if there is some way that we can fix the problem, we can ask God to show us. God can do the impossible, and with His power flowing through us and our confidence made strong, we can stand up to whatever gets in our way.

Pray:

Father God, You needn't prove anything to me. Please save me from my doubt and disbelief.

IS THAT YOU, GOD?

Read Hebrews 5:11–14

Key Verse:

Anyone who lives on milk cannot understand the teaching about being right with God. He is a baby.
HEBREWS 5:13 NLV

Understand:

- What do you think "milk" means in Hebrews 5:13?
- How well do you know the Bible? Do you read and study it daily?
- Are you able to discern God's voice from other thoughts?

Apply:

God wants us to *know* His voice. He wants such a close relationship with us that when He speaks inside our hearts, His voice is familiar. God doesn't need to prove anything to us. To know our Father's voice, we must earnestly seek Him.

Our key verse today compares some Christians to babies. They are immature in their knowledge of God's Word. To know God's voice, we need to be familiar with what's in both the Old and New

Testaments. It takes more than just reading the Bible. Along with reading, we should think about and meditate on its words. Sometimes while thinking, we will hear God's voice inside our hearts. He might reveal to us how something we've read in the Bible applies to our own lives. God's voice will never contradict what's in the Bible. This is another way we can test whether the voice is His. God's voice might repeat a thought multiple times, or a specific verse might suddenly pop into your head. His voice is gentle. It doesn't threaten or condemn. Being sure of God's voice leads to peace.

Is God speaking to you today? Spend some quiet time with Him and listen to your heart. Can you hear Him?

Pray:

Dear Lord, I don't want to be immature in my understanding of You. Help me to build a stronger relationship with You by reading and studying Your Word and learning to recognize Your voice.

WHAT DO YOU THINK OF ME?

Read John 12:37–43

Key Verse:

They loved to have the respect from men more than honor from God.
John 12:43 NLV

Understand:

- What do you think it means to have a hard heart toward Jesus?
- Do you worry about what others think of you?
- What do you think is God's opinion of you?

Apply:

In today's reading, many people had hardened their hearts toward Jesus. Remember, this was before His crucifixion and resurrection. The religious leaders didn't believe that Jesus was the Son of God, the Messiah, and the people had been taught to respect their opinions. There were some people, though, who did believe in Jesus, but they were afraid to say so. They cared more about being judged for their opinions than standing up for their beliefs.

Too often, we worry about what others might

think. We worry not only about what they would think if we shared our faith but also about how they might judge the ways we dress, talk, eat, act. . . We worry about being judged and found inferior or inadequate.

It dishonors God when we focus too much on the opinions of others. What matters is what God thinks of us. Proverbs 29:25 (MSG) says, "The fear of human opinion disables; trusting in GOD protects you from that." Putting too much value on what others think can lead to feeling poorly about ourselves, and that separates us from God.

Pray:

Lord God, I do worry sometimes about what others think of me. When I get dressed, I wonder if I look pretty enough. I don't share my thoughts on issues that might be unpopular, and I can be shy about sharing my faith. Forgive me, please, for putting too much value on what others think. What matters, Lord, is what You think of me.

FEAR NOT

Read Genesis 15:1-6

Key Verse:

After these things the word of the LORD came unto Abram in a vision, saying, Fear not, Abram: I am thy shield, and thy exceeding great reward.

GENESIS 15:1 KJV

Understand:

- Is fear a central theme in your life?
- Why do you think the words *fear not* appear so often in the Bible?

Apply:

Today's scripture reading is a familiar one. Abram (Abraham) worried because he didn't have a son. Then God came to him in a vision and said, "Fear not!" God promised Abram a son and a long line of descendants. "He took him outside and said, 'Now look up into the heavens and add up the stars, if you are able to number them.' Then He said to him, 'Your children and your children's children will be as many as the stars'" (Genesis 15:5 NLV).

Fear not. The first time these words appear in the King James Version is in Genesis 15:1. "Fear not" appears 63 times in the King James Bible, and the word *fear* shows up in 387 Old Testament verses and 114 New Testament verses. Think about that. Fear is a theme throughout the Bible. From the beginning, people have felt afraid, and God says, "Fear not."

Fear and worry are facts of life. But if you search for the word *fear* in the Bible, you will discover that God always helps His people overcome their worries and fears. He will do that for you too.

Tonight, go outside and look up at the stars. Imagine each one saying to you, "Fear not!" Be comforted and find peace in God's presence. God, the one who made the stars, is there watching over you.

Pray:

Dear God, thank You for reminding me that You always watch over me. I trust You to work out, for my good, everything that makes me worried and afraid.

WRITE IT DOWN

Read Revelation 21:1-5

Key Verse:

Then the One sitting on the throne said, "See! I am making all things new. Write, for these words are true and faithful."
REVELATION 21:5 NLV

Understand:

- Why do you think God told John to write down what He said?
- Do you worry about the end of the world?
- Have you tried journaling? If so, what did you learn about yourself?

Apply:

We worry about the world ending, but those who know God needn't be afraid. Revelation 21:1–5 presents a beautiful image of the end of the world as we know it. God will destroy all evil, and His children, those living and those who have died, will be ushered into a perfect world, the kind of world God intended for us to live in since the beginning. God gave this revelation to John, and He told John to write about it. "These words are true and faithful," God said.

Imagine the prophets, disciples, and scribes writing the Bible, all inspired by God, and every word faithful and true. They wrote what they saw, heard, and learned. The New Testament writers offered their thoughts on what they had learned from the ancient books and how it grew their faith.

Journaling is a great way to see your faith grow. When you write about your thoughts and apply what the Bible teaches, you not only release some of your worry but also build up your faith. Try it today. Start writing down your thoughts, your prayers, and the words God speaks to your heart. See where He leads you.

Pray:

Heavenly Father, for thousands of years, You encouraged men to write about You, and their words created the Bible. Please inspire me to write down my thoughts for the purpose of growing my faith and building a stronger relationship with You. Help me to apply what I know about You to my everyday life.

THE COMPANY WE KEEP

Read Psalm 26:1–7

Key Verses:

I scrub my hands with purest soap, then join hands with the others in the great circle, dancing around your altar, God, singing God-songs at the top of my lungs, telling God-stories.

Psalm 26:6–7 MSG

Understand:

- What kinds of people did David avoid spending time with?
- How can those you associate with affect you negatively?
- Are there people in your life who lead you to worry even more?

Apply:

Psalm 26 is another of David's prayers. The New Life Version of the Bible calls it the "Prayer of a Good Man." David had surrendered all to God. He was firm in his faith, and he asked God to make sure his faith stayed strong, always in step with Him. Then David spoke about his associations with others. He told God that he didn't hang out with "tricksters. . .thugs. . . gangsters. . .double-dealers" (verses 4–5 MSG). In other words, David didn't keep company with those who might lead him into sin or bring him down.

The company we keep is important. It's not good to associate with troublemakers, like those David wrote about. However, there are other types of troublemakers that David didn't mention. These individuals encourage us to worry and be afraid. Although it may not be their intention to lead us into feelings of anxiety and fear, spending time with them often leaves us feeling worse.

David spoke about washing away these troublemakers and joyfully dancing with others, "singing God-songs. . .[and] telling God-stories." When people bring us down, we can follow David's example by surrounding ourselves with positive people and changing the conversation to focus on the good and wonderful things of God.

Pray:

Dear God, guide me to examine the company I keep and to limit the time I spend with those who increase my feelings of worry and fear.

THINK OF ALL HE'S DONE

Read Amos 2:6–11

Key Verse:

"Yet think of all I did for them!"
Amos 2:9 TLB

Understand:

- Why was God angry with the Israelites?
- What are five wonderful things God has done for you?

Apply:

Amos was a common shepherd when God called him to deliver a message to the Israelites. They had settled in the Promised Land and prospered, but with their prosperity they had fallen away from God. While on the surface life looked good, many of Israel's people and leaders were corrupt, and this made God angry. He sent Amos to let the people know. "Think of all I did for them!" God said. He spoke to Amos about how He had led the Israelites out of Egypt to the Promised Land, removed those living there, and given the land to His people, and now the Israelites had forgotten Him.

Like the Israelites, in good times we sometimes forget about God. If our minds focus on prosperity and worldly things, God might give us a wake-up call, as He did the Israelites. He allowed them to face some worries so they would come back to Him for help.

God doesn't want us to live in worry and fear, but He also doesn't want us to focus more on our blessings than on Him. Whatever your reasons for worry, you can find peace by remembering all the good things God has done for you. Try making a list of your blessings at the end of each day. Focusing on God's goodness will help you feel less anxious.

Pray:

Almighty God, You have done so much for me! Your abundant blessings are new each day, and for each one I am grateful. Above all else, may I always remember Your goodness and be thankful.

MY EMPTY NEST

Read Ecclesiastes 7:8–10, 13–14

Key Verse:

Do not say, "Why were the days of the past better than these?" For it is not wise to ask this.
ECCLESIASTES 7:10 NLV

Understand:

- Do you often wish that things were as they used to be?
- Do you agree that "the end of something is better than its beginning" (Ecclesiastes 7:8 NLV)?

Apply:

Ecclesiastes 7:8 says, "The end of something is better than its beginning." But what if it's the end of something good? Women mourn when the last of their children moves out. The house is quiet yet filled with memories of babies crying, children playing, basketballs bouncing, musical instruments being practiced, teenagers whining and arguing. . . Where have those good days gone?

Recent empty nesters often experience a difficult time of transition, especially if it coincides with the beginning of retirement, the beginning of a new decade of middle age. . .the beginning of menopause! Sometimes beginnings are hard and uncomfortable. They leave us worrying about what's next and hoping that it's good.

About beginnings and endings, Ecclesiastes 7:14 (NLV) says, "God has made the one as well as the other, so that man can never know what is going to happen." But "not knowing" doesn't have to lead to dread. We can view an empty nest with joyful expectations for our children and for our future. Now, it's time to ask God to make straight not only our children's paths but our own.

God is inviting you into this new phase of your life and promising to lead you. Will you accept His invitation? If so, ask Him to open the door to what's next.

Pray:

Father, there is a season for everything. Help me to view each ending as a new beginning, and lead me in the way I should go.

THE WARRIOR JUDGE

Read Judges 4:4–9

Key Verse:

She held court under the Palm of Deborah between Ramah and Bethel in the hill country of Ephraim, and the Israelites went up to her to have their disputes decided.

Judges 4:5 NIV

Understand:

- What do you think made Deborah different from other women of her time?
- What one word might best describe Deborah's character?

Apply:

Deborah lived in a world dominated by men. Like Moses and Samuel, she was both a prophet and a judge—an unusual role for a woman of her time. Deborah held court under a palm tree, where she resolved disputes brought to her by the Israelites. Along with being a judge, she was also a military leader and a warrior. Deborah inspired her troops and led them into battle with the confidence that God would grant her a victory. She truly embodied strength.

When we worry about not being strong enough, we can look to Deborah as an example. She relied on God for strength, was confident in her faith, and was unafraid. In everything she did, Deborah marched forward with the assurance that God was with her, would guide her, and would help her succeed.

In the early 1970s, singer-songwriter Helen Reddy recorded her hit song "I Am Woman." The lyrics describe a woman who gained wisdom through hurt and pain, ultimately coming back even stronger. She understood that while circumstances might bend her, she would not be broken. We can imagine Deborah as that kind of woman.

We are all like Deborah—women warriors. We may not have physical strength, but we can have spiritual strength. When we rely on God for our strength, we can tackle every obstacle with determination.

Pray:

Dear God, please bless me with
a strong and confident spirit,
one that is led and inspired by You.

LOOKING FOR LOVE

Read 1 Corinthians 13:1-8

Key Verse:

If I speak with human eloquence and angelic ecstasy but don't love, I'm nothing but the creaking of a rusty gate.
1 Corinthians 13:1 MSG

Understand:

- How would you define love?
- When looking for a potential husband, what personality traits top/topped your list?

Apply:

The abundance of dating apps and social media sites proves that women (and men) are looking for love. Some women worry that they might never find it. But maybe they are looking for the wrong things in the wrong places.

In today's reading, Paul provided a helpful account of what to look for in love:

- Love never gives up.
- Love cares more for others than for self.
- Love doesn't want what it doesn't have.

- Love doesn't strut,
- Doesn't have a swelled head,
- Doesn't force itself on others,
- Isn't always "me first,"
- Doesn't fly off the handle,
- Doesn't keep score of the sins of others,
- Doesn't revel when others grovel,
- Takes pleasure in the flowering of truth,
- Puts up with anything,
- Trusts God always,
- Always looks for the best,
- Never looks back,
- But keeps going to the end. (1 Corinthians 13:4–7 MSG)

This biblical list is a good reference when looking for love that will last. Instead of worrying about finding love, trust God and pray. He knows what you want but also what you need. God understands everything about love because He *is* love (1 John 4:8).

Pray:

Father, if it is Your will for me to marry, please match me with the man You have chosen for me. Bless me with the gift of love.

THE SINGLE LIFE

Read 1 Corinthians 7:32–35

Key Verse:

I am saying this to help you, not to try to keep you from marrying. I want you to do whatever will help you serve the Lord best, with as few other things as possible to distract your attention from him.

1 Corinthians 7:35 TLB

Understand:

- What have you learned about life from the single people you know?
- Are you (or could you be) content staying single?

Apply:

Some women worry about being single and others are content. In 1 Corinthians 7, Paul, who was single, had much to say about both lifestyles:

"In times like these [when Christians are persecuted] I think it is best for a person to remain unmarried. . . . But if you men decide to go ahead anyway and get married now, it is all right; and if a girl gets married in times like these, it is no sin. However, marriage will bring extra problems that I wish you didn't have to face right now" (verses 26,

28 TLB). "I wish everyone could get along without marrying, just as I do. But we are not all the same. God gives some the gift of a husband or wife, and others he gives the gift of being able to stay happily unmarried" (verse 7 TLB). "But be sure in deciding these matters that you are living as God intended, marrying or not marrying in accordance with God's direction and help, and accepting whatever situation God has put you into" (verse 17 TLB).

Being single might not be your choice, but it needn't be your worry. God has a plan for us all, whether single or married, and it includes serving others. Happiness comes from focusing on Him.

Pray:

Lord, whatever Your plan for me, may I find happiness and contentment by accepting it, putting You first, and serving others.

LONELINESS

Read Psalm 25:16–21

Key Verse:

Turn to me and be gracious to me,
for I am lonely and afflicted.
Psalm 25:16 NIV

Understand:

- Have you ever experienced intense loneliness?
- Do you feel lonely right now?
- Name three things you can do to overcome loneliness.

Apply:

It is rare for someone never to have experienced loneliness. It comes in many forms. A child attending a new school feels lonely until she makes friends. A young woman experiences loneliness when a job change requires moving to a city where she doesn't know anyone. Mothers feel lonely when their children grow up and leave home, and widows encounter intense loneliness when their husbands die. We worry about being alone. Loneliness comes and goes. It is present in all stages of life. Loneliness can be a big worry if we dwell on it.

David, in the Bible, felt lonely when hiding from his enemies. In today's scripture passage, he cried out to God, asking Him to take his loneliness away. David always found refuge in the Lord and hope in Him.

If anyone understands our loneliness, Jesus does. Imagine how alone He felt in those last days when His friends had all abandoned Him and most people hated Him. While suffering the intense burden of our sins, He cried out to His Father, "My God, my God, why hast thou forsaken me?" (Mark 15:34 KJV).

Whatever causes you to feel lonely, trust in the Lord. Trust Jesus to meet all your needs. Talk with Him because He is your friend; He understands.

Pray:

Jesus, I feel so alone. I need You, my Savior and my friend. Come and comfort me. Lead me out of my loneliness and deliver me to a place of peace, fellowship, and joy.

SICKNESS AND WORRY

Read 2 Kings 20:1–7

Key Verse:

"Go back and tell Hezekiah, the ruler of my people, 'This is what the LORD, the God of your father David, says: I have heard your prayer and seen your tears; I will heal you.'"

2 KINGS 20:5 NIV

Understand:

- Do you worry about becoming terminally ill?
- How would you pray if you faced a life-threatening illness?

Apply:

One of the greatest worries is a terminal illness. Hezekiah was in that situation. In desperation, he prayed, "Remember, LORD, how I have walked before you faithfully and with wholehearted devotion and have done what is good in your eyes," and then "wept bitterly" (2 Kings 20:3 NIV). God healed Hezekiah, proof that God can and does work miracles. But what if healing doesn't happen?

A Christian author facing terminal cancer said to her friend, "Healing here or in heaven—either way, I win." She had prayed persistently through phases of begging for her life, seeking peace, and, eventually, accepting God's will, knowing that whatever happened she would be okay. God hears our prayers. He sees our tears, and He always brings healing, sometimes here and sometimes in heaven. Our earthly bodies are temporary, but our souls are eternal.

We can hope. We should never stop praying to face each day with strength. Only God knows which day will be our last. In the meantime, we can try to live each day to its fullest and soak up all the love surrounding us. The Holy Spirit will help us know how to pray, and He will always pray for us if we are unable.

Pray:

Lord, I worry about cancer and other terminal illnesses. Only You know if that will happen to me, so help me not to be afraid of the unknown. Whatever happens, I will trust You to lead me. Today, I am alive! Thank You, God, for the gift of life.

LET YOUR FEELINGS SHOW

Read Romans 12:12-16

Key Verse:

Rejoice with those who rejoice;
mourn with those who mourn.
ROMANS 12:15 NIV

Understand:

- Is it difficult for you to allow others to see when you are worried or afraid?
- How might sharing your emotions be helpful to yourself and others?

Apply:

Romans 12:12–16 is packed with good advice. A gem hidden in it is Romans 12:15, "Rejoice with those who rejoice; mourn with those who mourn."

We sometimes put on a happy face and hide our emotions. It's not necessarily a bad thing to put on a happy face when we're feeling unhappy inside. But doing so habitually is a way of masking our feelings. One big step in overcoming worry and anxiety is letting others know how we feel.

Pride can keep us from sharing our emotions. But there's no shame in allowing our feelings to show. We all feel worried, unsure, powerless, angry, afraid. . . Sharing our emotions can relieve stress, encourage helpful advice, and provide empathy. Keeping negative feelings bottled up inside can lead to increased anxiety and feelings of hopelessness.

The Bible says that Ezra, a priest in his time, openly confessed sin and guilt to God; and when the Israelites saw, they empathized and gathered around him and wept bitterly with him (Ezra 10:1). This is what God calls us to do, to allow others to see our emotions and to show us empathy. As Christians, we are to hold each other up in bad times and rejoice with one another in good times.

Acknowledge your emotions for what they are. Then ask God to help you reveal your feelings in ways that are not hurtful but peaceful and beneficial to yourself and others.

Pray:

Dear God, help me to be vulnerable around my Christian friends, allowing my feelings to show. Let my heart be open to receiving their encouragement and empathy.

WHY PRAY MORE?

Read Colossians 4:2–4

Key Verse:

You must keep praying.
Keep watching! Be thankful always.
COLOSSIANS 4:2 NLV

Understand:

- Have you been praying often throughout each day?
- How can praying more help you worry less?

Apply:

Why should we pray even more? There are many reasons. Praying more. . .

- leads us nearer to God and helps us form a loving relationship with Him
- encourages us to talk with Him throughout the day
- helps us focus on Him instead of our troubles
- teaches us to surrender our problems to Him

- helps us put into words our worries and fears instead of overthinking them
- guides us to discover what is at the root of our worries
- allows us to experience God working in our lives
- builds our trust in Him
- improves our mood
- brings us peace

When Paul wrote Colossians, he was in prison for preaching about Jesus. Although his body was locked in a cell, his soul was set free through prayer and his faith in the Lord. Worry is a prison for the soul, and Satan is the jailer. Satan has no power over our worries when, like Paul, we pray more and put our trust in God.

Keep praying. Keep watching! Be thankful always to the Lord your God, who promises to bring you peace.

Pray:

Heavenly Father, I want to be a woman of prayer. Awaken my desire to talk with You more often. Open my eyes to see that You are with me wherever I go and whatever I do. Bless me, O Lord. Set me free from my worries as I surrender them all to You.

IS WORRY A CHOICE?

Read Luke 12:22-32

Key Verses:

"Which of you can make yourself a little taller by worrying? If you cannot do that which is so little, why do you worry about other things?"
LUKE 12:25–26 NLV

Understand:

- What have you learned about worry from this Bible study?
- Name several things you can do to worry less.

Apply:

Worry is a characteristic of being human. It becomes a problem, though, when our worries overpower our faith in God's ability to solve them. The more we dwell on our troubles, the less we rely on God.

Is worry a choice? Probably not. But we can choose how we handle worry. Here are ten tips that will help:

1. As soon as you begin to worry, start worshipping and praising God.
2. Be thankful for the many ways God has helped you.

3. Pray, and pray some more.
4. Identify the root cause of your worry.
5. Replace thoughts of the worst possible outcome with the best-ever outcome.
6. Surrender your worries to God and keep on surrendering them.
7. Trust God to meet all your needs.
8. Seek advice from wise Christian friends.
9. Keep your mind busy to turn your thoughts away from your worries.
10. Build up your faith by studying God's Word and memorizing scripture.

Remember—God is in control, and He loves you. You don't have to rely on your strength alone, because His strength is working through you. Find peace in God each day as you continue to practice worrying less and praying more.

Pray:

Dear God, thank You for lifting the burden of worry from my shoulders. Whatever trouble or obstacle I face, I have faith that with Your help I will overcome it. You, my almighty and all-powerful God, can do anything! Amen.

ABOUT THE AUTHOR

Jean Fischer is a bestselling author of Christian books for children and adults. She has written several devotional books for Barbour Publishing, including *100 Extraordinary Stories for Courageous Girls*. A nature lover, Jean lives in southeast Wisconsin, where she enjoys flower gardening, bird-watching, and maintaining a small urban wildlife habitat in her backyard.